A Return to the 'Boro

A Return to the 'Boro

Life in a Southern Town during Depression and War

George G. Suggs, Jr.

Library of Congress Control Number:		2017905711
ISBN:	Hardcover	978-1-5434-1597-1
	Softcover	978-1-5434-1596-4
	eBook	978-1-5434-1595-7

Print information available on the last page.

Rev. date: 04/17/2017

To order additional copies of this book, contact:
Xlibris
1-888-795-4274
www.Xlibris.com
Orders@Xlibris.com
759423

CONTENTS

To The People Of Bladenboro, North Carolina

And Vicinity

Introduction

Today the Town of Bladenboro, North Carolina as it existed in the thirties and forties no longer exists. Ironically, these tumultuous decades, which were scarred by the Great Depression and World War II, were high-water marks in the life of this once thriving village tucked away on the edge of Bryant Swamp in the southern portion of Bladen County, North Carolina. Empty streets that once were thronged with people standing shoulder to shoulder on weekends, empty or demolished stores that once catered to the demands of scores of patrons, empty lots where diverse, small shops once stood and thrived, a partially demolished textile mill complex that once employed hundreds of workers–are all stark reminders that what had been a robust and dynamic town is no more. For one who grew up in this bustling community of yesterday–and who loved it–it is no consolation to know that the slow, general deterioration of small towns that has occurred is not unique to Bladenboro. The phenomenon of small-town decline is nationwide as more and more people have been drawn into the orbit of big cities and the nation's agricultural and industrial economy has undergone a metamorphosis that has extensively damaged small-towns and their residents. Nevertheless, even from a distance, watching the demise of one's hometown is both difficult and sad.

Entering Bladenboro from the west along NC 211, an old-timer who lived through the town's most active era during depression and war is immediately struck by the physical changes that have occurred there, particularly in the town's major industrial enterprise, the Bladenboro Cotton Mills, formerly Bladen County's largest employer. The most startling change is the absence of the company's "New" mill with its water tank where hundreds of operatives–including my father who tended a set of frames there for fourteen years–worked first eleven and then eight-hour shifts tending the scores of cards, slubbers, speeders, twisters, spinning, and warp machines that filled its spacious length of brick and heart lumber later salvaged and used elsewhere. Equally conspicuous by its absence is the "New" mill village, a double row of approximately twelve traditional, company-owned houses, that were built near the west end of the mill. Formerly rented by workers, these houses were later given away by the company for removal, destroyed for salvage, or, in some cases, became victims of arson. Close to the former village where in the forties the mill company had built a new baseball park for its mill team, the Spinners, a new government subsidized block of small duplexes has replaced the facility. And the former site of the demolished "New" mill is now covered in rows of manufactured houses, a poor substitute for the hundreds of jobs lost with the sale and destruction of the mill.

Farther east on NC 211 and just beyond a former mill pond that separated the "New" from the "Old" mill with its towering smoke stack, the empty "Old" mill, its din of noise from whirring machines now silenced, remains intact but with substantial structural changes. The windows where workers once leaned out for a breath of fresh air and temporary relief from the pervasive noise and air-borne lint that saturated the interior, are now bricked in. The lofty stack, long in disuse and now just a symbolic reminder of what was once a thriving enterprise, remains soaring with little outward change, its attached loud whistle that summoned workers to their jobs now silent. The company store where day workers once thronged during shift changes and where families bought groceries and other items, a building that once stood independently at the east end of the "Old" mill, has now been incorporated by its new owners into the mill and is structurally invisible. And the "Old" mill village with its scores of families and rows of company-owned houses that made it much larger than the "New" mill village is also gone, its site now filled with numerous government subsidized, small brick duplexes. Other than the "Old" mill structure, little physically remains of a once thriving textile industry with its two villages that provided a livelihood for hundreds of workers and their families. Time and evolutionary change have erased the world of both the Bladenboro Cotton Mills and the mill hands who worked there.

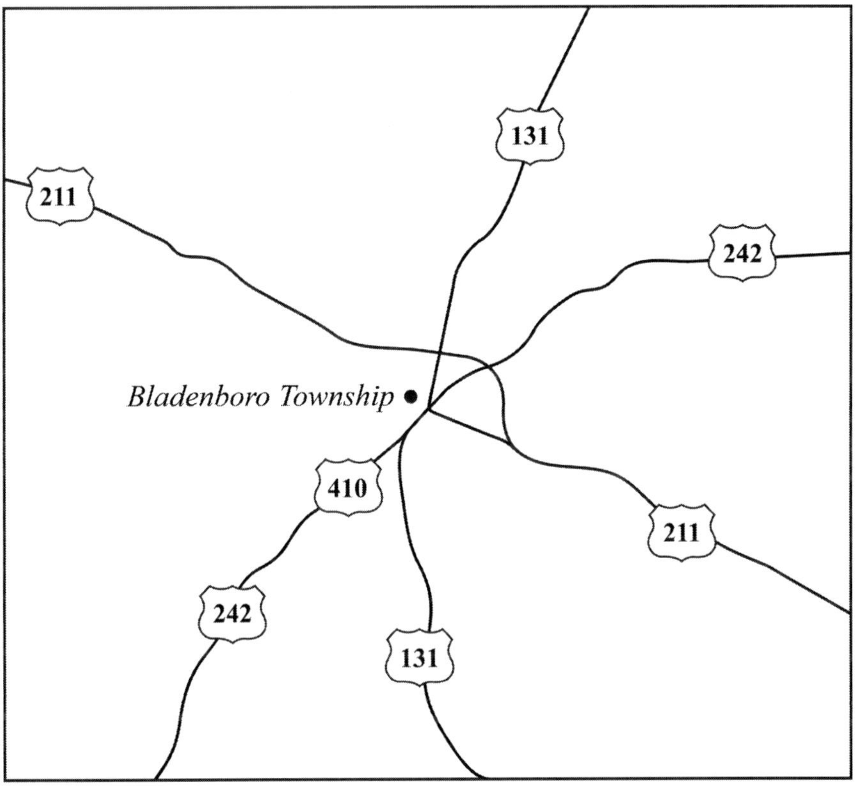

Credit: Whitney Mortimer

Another conspicuous change that an old timer notes when entering Bladenboro from the west on NC 211 is the major changes in the community of Pine Ridge. During the thirties and forties, Pine Ridge (located across NC 211 and the Seaboard Railroad and facing the front of the "New" mill) had very few homes. In 1935 when my family built there, only three homes existed on the site. In sharp contrast to the disappearance of the nearby "New" mill village, Pine Ridge has flourished and now has dozens of small, modest homes constructed over the past seventy-five years. Following NC 211 past the "Old" mill into Bladenboro, a distance of less than a mile, other major changes have occurred. Numerous small enterprises that once catered to mill workers and their families en route on foot to town have disappeared: stores owned during the thirties and forties by Bud Edwards, Bill and Molly Cain, Frank Guyton, Caz Deaver, A. C. Hardin, Cary Dowless, Smithy Edwards, and Albert Thompson. And also gone are a number of roadside homes owned by the Adcoxes, Suggses, Kinlaws, Stubbs, Shipman, F. Guyton, Deavers, Hardins, Paits, Thompsons, Dowlesses, E. Guytons, and Bryant families. They have been replaced by other small enterprises–a new Dollar Store, the Cape Fear Medical, a new fire station, a Boz Supermarket, a Kangaroo gas station, a washerette, and a florist. Even so, time has not been kind to the Bladenboro's west end on NC 211 as it existed in the thirties and forties. The old has been devastated by changes that have not always been for the better.

If an old timer enters Bladenboro from the east on NC 211, the physical changes appear less obvious but nevertheless significant. Entrance from this direction takes one through what was once called the "colored" section of town. There many African-Americans lived together with a few scattered white families such as that of D. H. Russ, owner of a downtown general store, and Grover Pait, owner of a small trucking firm located adjacent to his home. As on west NC 211, the homes of residents rested extremely close to the roadway. Located on this half-mile stretch of NC 211 was segregated Spaulding-Monroe school for African-American children–still there but now integrated–and the active First Baptist Church and the AME Church, both African-American in their membership. These churches have remained enduring landmarks for the Black community within Bladenboro.

Time has also brought changes to this area. Pait's trucking firm no longer exists. Nor does a once flourishing cotton-ginning business situated directly across NC 211 from the AME Church. The gin, like the cotton mills an extremely valuable economic asset to the town and region, processed locally produced cotton, then a major commercial crop of most farmers in Bladen County, and supplied raw cotton to the nearby Bladenboro Cotton Mills and other area yarn mills. Although the cotton gin itself was located closer to the siding of the Seaboard Railroad than to the highway, the company's warehouses, where it stored its inventory of five-hundred pound bales of cotton prior to shipment to the local textile mills or elsewhere, extended close to NC 211. Like the textile mills of west Bladenboro, the cotton gin and its warehouses have not been replaced by an industrial concern of comparable economic value to the community. However, on the fringe of this once industrial location, several changes have occurred that provide significant benefits for the residents of Bladenboro and the surrounding area. A small, architecturally interesting medical facility, a Dollar Store, a new postoffice, a coin-operated laundry, and a new bank have been built that have changed the structural appearance of the immediate east entrance into Bladenboro along NC 211. These new concerns have partially offset the loss of the trucking and the cotton ginning firms.

Entering Bladenboro along NC 410 (Chadbourn road) & NC 131 (Whiteville road) from the south, one also encounters substantial changes from the decades of the thirties and forties. On the immediate approach to town on NC 410, facing the highway are fine homes that were built after World War II on formerly wooded sites. On the periphery of town, the Bridger Cemetery has experienced a major enlargement, facelift and a name change. It is now called Pine Crest Cemetery, perhaps reflecting the major social changes that occurred with the demise of the town's predominant economic concerns, such as the textile, cotton ginning, banking, and mercantile interests, once extensively controlled by members of the Bridger family. Perhaps the most conspicuous change has occurred in the triangular area south of where NC 410 and NC 131 converge. For it is here that the Bladenboro Public Schools, once reported to be the largest consolidated school system in the state during the thirties and forties, continue to be located. Like the Spaulding-Monroe school on NC 211, it was then segregated and enrolled only white students. At that time, there was a two-storied elementary building, a single-storied high-school building, a wooden gymnasium, and a grandstand with a ball park surrounded by a wooden fence. Today, the school's physical plant and its campus have been radically changed. The wooden gymnasium, the grandstand, and the wooden fence are gone, replaced by a modern gymnasium and athletic field with lights. The shell of the old high school has been incorporated into a modern middle school, and across adjacent NC 131 a new elementary school exists. The old elementary school remains but is not used for educational purposes. However, rather than raze it, at great expense and much volunteer work historically minded citizens have converted it into a thriving museum that is now one of the town's greatest assets. And, of course, the schools are no longer segregated as they once were. White and black students now attend classes together. These changes have made the south entrance into Bladenboro very different from the decades of depression and war.

When entering Bladenboro from the north either on NC 410 (Dublin road) or NC 242 (Elizabethtown road) before they merge, one finds that there is also significant change from the decade of the thirties and forties. For example, a new NC 211 bypass has been built that diverts traffic, particularly truck traffic, around downtown Bladenboro. Named for Lt/Cdr Frank Elkins, a local, naval pilot who was shot down and lost during the Vietnam War, the bypass must be crossed by a traveler entering town by either road from the north. And along its northern periphery are located several of the town's later ongoing businesses. On NC 242 before its convergence with NC 410 prior to entering town, except for a public housing development, a convenience store, and the removal of a drive-in theater once owned by Curtis Cain there has been little change worth noting. Landmarks such as Frank Hester's air strip and the nearby African-American cemetery yet remain as carry overs from the past.

But in the approach to town along NC 410, one finds more contrast with yesteryear. From Zion Hill Baptist Church to the intersection with the bypass, what once was farm land is now dotted with modern homes and a few business concerns. And immediately upon crossing the bypass, a Hardees fast-food restaurant, a Dollar Store, a nursery, and a new convenience store now occupy a formerly wooded area and the former site of a saw mill. Until its convergence with NC 242, other than the closing of Frank Hester's garage and the construction of a few homes and a funeral home little has changed on NC 410.

It is in the business section of Bladenboro itself where the greatest changes have occurred, changes that expose a decades long, continuing decline that, if not halted, will result in the further demise of the town as a viable, functioning commercial entity. In contrast to the economic vitality found during the decades of depression and war and the encouraging developments on roads leading into town, there is little today that suggests anything other than a negative economic comparison with the past. If one travels north from the Bladenboro Public Schools down Main Street (formerly Front Street) past the First Baptist Church of Bladenboro to the Seaboard Railroad tracks, he will find both renovated old and new beautiful homes, with some of the older homes now in far better shape than in the thirties and forties. (This street was formerly known as the "Street of Beautiful Homes".) A new, residential development located behind the First Baptist Church of Bladenboro and new houses on Ash Street (formerly Back Street) that runs parallel to Main Street form the major residential section of the town. It is upon crossing the Seaboard tracks into the business section that the commercial changes and contrast with the thirties and forties on Main Street becomes so clearly evident.

On its east side, gone is the business of the Bridger Corporation Store, the largest and leading mercantile establishment with its row of wooden warehouses (destroyed by fire) that met the needs of hundreds of local residents and farmers. Gone is Henry White's adjacent livery stables that supplied Missouri mules and wagons to local farmers. Gone is Theron Pait's little wooden office that housed a fledgling Savings and Loan business. Gone is M. Nance's food stand where he and his wife sold hamburgers, hot dogs, fish sandwiches, and soft drinks to the Saturday throngs of people. Gone is W. G. Fussell's Wonet Theater (formerly the Lyric Theater) that provided the area's major entertainment. Gone is Vaught's Cash Store. Gone are Dr. S. S. Hutchinson's Drug Store and backroom offices. Gone is the corner gas station operated by Arthur Watterson. And gone is James A. Bridger's Bridger Motor Company where skilled mechanics worked and Ford automobiles were sold. In a few cases, even the buildings where these businesses were located have been demolished; for example, the Bridger Motor Company, Watterson's gas station, the Wonet Theater, and White's livery stables. Replacements on the eastside of Main are limited to a hardware store, the Medicine Shop and Helms Optometry, and an antique shop in the former Bridger Corporation Store.

Reversing course from the bridge over Bryant Swamp and heading south on Main street's westside, gone is a Western Auto Store and the Hussey Brothers Grocery (formerly Oz Hester's bicycle and repair shop). Gone is the corner of the Hutchinson block that was once part of a hotel that serviced traveling salesmen and was later the site of several businesses including restaurants (for example, two operated by Allie Page) and a variety store. Gone is the old Lyric Theater that W. G. Fussell closed when opening the Wonet directly across Main Street, and the small restaurant later at that site run by Allie Page and her daughters. Gone is the wooden Presbyterian Church that occupied a conspicuous lot in downtown Bladenboro. Gone are a number of businesses making up the Bridger block. Gone is the Bank of Bladenboro that had remained open during the throes of the Great Depression. Gone is Dr. Vance's dental office above the bank (probably the first professional dental practice in Bladenboro). Gone is Ed Lewis's furniture store and upstairs casket shop. Gone is Tom Hale's grocery store (a very minor competitor to the Bridger Corporation Store directly across Main Street). Gone is Charley Bell Ward's barber shop. Gone is the Bridger Drug Store that C. A. Shaw managed for decades and was the meeting place of the Bladenboro Intellectual Club. Gone are the medical offices of Dr. Dewey H. Bridger, Sr. located in the back of the drugstore. Gone are the upstairs corporate offices of the Bladenboro Cotton Mills. And, crossing the railroad tracks, gone are the waiting rooms and depot of the Seaboard Railroad where for years Woody Hilburn managed both passenger and freight service from a small cramped office while listening to the constant clicking of morse code messages concerning rail traffic. Other than the demolition of the corner of the Hutchinson block and the Presbyterian Church, the structures on the westside of Main Street between the stoplight and the Seaboard tracks have remained intact. However, in the optimistic post-World War II years, several contiguous stores were built on the large lot that had been vacated with the removal of the Presbyterian church and on the empty lot adjacent to the Bank of Bladenboro. With the possible exception of Steve Inman's Diamond Dave's Restaurant, Hickman's Insurance Co., a HUD office, and several thrift stores, little remains on the west side of Main Street.

One of the most commercially viable section of Bladenboro in the depression and war years–and even today–was the section on NC 211 that lay west between the stoplight and the Bryant Swamp bridge. From the stoplight westward on the north side, James Albert Bridger had built a row of small contiguous shops, backs to the swamp, that he leased to various small entrepreneurs. Oz Hester's repair shop, Dan Freeman's clothing store, D. H. Russ grocery, Azzie Harding's barber shop, Pelo's pool hall, Searles Five and Dime (later Truett Freeman's jewelry store), Mrs. Buie's coffee shop, a restaurant, a wartime shoe repair shop, and other small businesses. Separated from the Bridger block was gasoline station. Before the end of the forties, there was added a Collins' department store and A. A. White's Kaiser-Fraser dealership, which White later moved to Tabor City. And eastward on the south side back from the bridge to the stoplight were Walter Elmore's City Service gas station and garage, another gas station, the town jail, Taylor's grocery store (later Hussey Brothers' Grocery), Blanco Duvall's store and fish market, Allie Page's restaurant as a part of the Hutchinson Block. Like the rest of Bladenboro, Friday afternoons and Saturdays were usually filled with smoking and tobacco-chewing farmers and textile workers who crowded the limited sidewalks and dodged moving cars and trucks while cris-crossing NC 211 to shop in these small stores. Today, all the above businesses are gone, as well as the swarm of people who provided the Friday and Saturday frenzy of street activity, all victims of time. The buildings housing the stores have deteriorated and some have been removed leaving conspicuous gaps. Nevertheless, a few entrepreneurs continue to struggle in this section of town that has seen better days.

If one considers the economic conditions that exist now in the Twenty-first Century, it is difficult to conclude that there will ever be a revitalization of Bladenboro to the level of economic life prevailing in the thirties and forties. In the United States since the ending of World War II, new technologies and corporate greed feeding off cheap overseas labor has readily victimized the Southern textile industry of the mid-Twentieth Century with its scores of family-owned cotton and fabric mills that had so long sustained the economic life of mill families and many small towns like Bladenboro. The Bladenboro Cotton Mills and its hundred of employees were victims of these developments. Technological displacement and the shipment of remaining textile jobs elsewhere in order to enhance profits by exploiting cheap labor sounded the death knell to a vital Southern industry. In Bladenboro where the flow of wages from mill workers constantly refreshed the local economy, their disappearance over time had an extremely negative impact on the town's economic life. More and more the local economy was forced to depend upon the success or failure of agriculture that was also being hurt by growing restrictions on cash crops like tobacco production. And when accelerating globalization set in that drained even more of America's productive industries overseas–for example, steel, shoes, and furniture–it became even more difficult to attract industrial enterprises that employed substantial numbers of workers into the nation's small towns like Bladenboro.

Thus, despite repeated and energetic campaigns of local citizens who love the town to renew and boost its economic status and provide for broad-based livelihoods, sadly the likelihood of Bladenboro recapturing the heady days of the thirties and forties is not promising. For those of us who grew up there and remember its former vitality–even during depression and war–the town's core demise and its apparently bleak future are disheartening to contemplate. Unfortunately, like so many other similar, small towns, Bladenboro has been caught up in a maelstrom of external developments that have forced changes beyond the control of its citizens. Although evolving into something new, it may never return to what it was, that is, to the thriving town that lives only in the memory of many of its older citizens and former residents.

The reader should keep in mind that what follows is a work of memory. It is not–and is not intended to be–a thoroughly researched historical work that examines the institutional anatomy of the Town of Bladenboro. For example, there is no reference to town government and its operations. And although it is full of nostalgia, it should not be read as a longing for the return of the lifestyle and relationships of the thirties and forties, that is, a return to the good old days. The book is simply what it purports to be–reflections on growing up in a thriving town whose people had enormous influence on the early life and development of the author. It must also be noted that the memories of others concerning some of the following may be different from his reflections. It would be surprising were they not.

Chapter 1

Class Structure

One could not grow up in Bladenboro without realizing that its people related to each other along loosely defined class lines. This perception was probably strongest among those of us who occupied the lower rungs of the social ladder and who, if then asked to do so, would have found it difficult to explain our simple insights into class in ways intelligible to a modern sociologist. But the differences that separated us, both imagined and real, often found unfortunate expression in dwarfed and stunted lives. For class divisions distorted self-concepts, limited horizons and vistas, and made it difficult to dream of lives that measured up to our felt potential. All this was made worse by the prevalence of "hard times" in the thirties and war in the forties which added to the vague frustrations that class awareness generated. But, paradoxically, it was World War II that set the stage for substantial changes in group relationships in Bladenboro and the surrounding countryside. With the return of veterans from all over the world, what once had been acceptable was no longer tolerable. Things were never really the same again. The old system faded away in the surge of less deferential attitudes and postwar opportunities.

The social structure in the thirties was determined by one or a combination of the following considerations--family, occupation, income, race, religion, home ownership and location, and possibly others. While these factors helped to establish one's status and/or class identity, some of them also worked to ameliorate the ill effects produced by our separation from each other. The marriage of persons from different classes, for example, produced inter-family networking that reduced somewhat the harshness of class relationships. Although a rare occurrence in the thirties and forties, such cross-over marriages were less rare in the fifties and sixties when even biracial marriages began to occur. Or, a person with two occupations, such as farming and working in the local cotton mills, might escape an indelible identification with either group. Such an individual had the luxury of choice. But in spite of divisions reflecting class, there was evidence of social mobility, vertical and horizontal. For the most part, however, a person tended to remain in whatever group he found himself, that is, to "stay with his own kind." In retrospect, it seems that the social structure had four clearly identifiable strata which, for want of a better term, I will refer to as classes. These were the Blacks, Lint-Heads, Bo'Weevils and Front-Streeters. However, it would be a serious error to suggest that these were completely homogenous groups. They were not. Within each was a wide range of differences produced by a wide variety of circumstances.

Blacks occupied the lowest rung of the local social system, just as they did in the larger segregated society of the South where legally enforced separation of the races in schools, public conveyances, marriages, and so on, defined their official status. In the context of white racial attitudes, it was therefore natural that blacks in Bladenboro should rest at the bottom of the social structure. However, the many necessary contacts between the races often reduced the antagonism generated by legal discrimination and separation.

Humane relationships between blacks and whites based on mutual respect were not uncommon. Even so, among local whites there was generally no question concerning the low status of blacks. That status was determined solely by color. Their achievements, education, character, wealth, and craftsmanship were conspicuously ignored or diminished because of race. In the final analysis, according to conventional wisdom, a black was a black. In the order of things, the rightful "place" of a black was at the bottom. No one believed this more firmly than lower-class whites who had a compelling need to believe that there were others lower than themselves.

Local whites, of course, made a great mistake when they lumped all blacks together simply because of their color, for one did not have to be an astute social analyst to note the vast differences among them.

Their great diversity was especially evident in the kinds of occupations they pursued. Although the prevailing segregated educational system was generally disastrous for blacks, it nevertheless provided them with professional opportunities as administrators and teachers. Blacks ran their schools (for example, Spaulding-Monroe), a fact which gave these educators a superior status among blacks and recognized even among those whites who prized education. As a boy selling yard brooms from door to door in the black section of town, I visited the home of a black principal who answered my knock on the door dressed in a nice business suit. Today as an adult I recall my childish surprise at unexpectedly finding a black man so finely dressed.

In my boyish mind, the suit immediately identified the man as someone a cut-above-average. Just as the type of clothes worn by cotton mill workers roughly defined their status in the mills, to me the suit marked the principal as a man of importance. By virtue of education, position and a steady, although low salary, black educators ranked at the top of their local class. In the absence of race, their interests would have been completely compatible with their counterparts in the town's white school system. For, except for race, their lots were essentially the same.

Ministers, businessmen, and craftsmen also ranked high in status among blacks. Although I never personally knew any black ministers it was evident that they were held in high esteem and were very influential. Like their white opposites who served most of the local churches, black ministers, after receiving the "call," labored at other occupations to support themselves. Local congregations--black or white--generally could not afford "full-time," educated, seminary-trained ministers. Thus local congregations were served by men "filled with the spirit" and little else. Aunt Clara Tyler lived for awhile next door to the black St. Luke AME church on east NC 211 in the section derogatorily called the "quarters," a portion of which, in spite of the name, was well integrated. On Sunday evenings during the summer, we sat on her front porch and listened and observed the lively services in the church. After such experiences, one could neither doubt the profound influence of black ministers on their congregations nor their status as leaders.

The town had several black businessmen who also enjoyed higher status. For awhile, James Robinson operated one of the two dry-cleaning establishment in town. Because of the quality of his work, the mill-owning white collar residents on Front Street continued to patronize

Robinson's business even after Jodie Bennett, a white, open a new dry cleaners in competition. And blacks owned a "funeral parlor" and a barbershop on NC 211 east of the town's only stoplight that met the needs of the black community for these services. Recognized as being among the finest brick masons in the area were Booker T. Ruffin and his brother whose craftsmanship was in demand from whites as well as blacks. They were conspicuous for their skill and the income they derived from it. B. J. Lacy was another extremely able brick mason whose work was sought by both blacks and whites. Much later in the eighties Lacy became a well-known entrepreneur, a contractor in concrete who became very successful by exploiting minority set-asides on government projects. Lacy consulted and hired as a supervisor George Kelly, my cousin Alma's husband, on several projects he had won through government intervention.

The "hard times" of the thirties clobbered rank-and-file blacks whose livelihood depended solely upon their labor. In the matter of jobs, the "pickings" were slimmer for them than for whites. Except for yard work, blacks were not employed in the Bladenboro Cotton Mills, the primary employer of the town. Consequently, some black females became domestics for Front-Street residents and, occasionally, even for mill families beset with sickness. Some worked steadily as washerwomen (for example, Sofia [Sofa] Hester), having a clientele that ranged from the mill villages to Front Street. In both occupations, the pay was low. Black males worked at whatever jobs they could find but usually at manual labor. Like their white counterparts, some found employment after 1935 on Works Progress Administration (WPA), although these jobs were not plentiful for blacks or whites.

A few lucked into jobs with the Seaboard Railroad that were physically demanding but were considered "good" jobs because they provided steady employment. Blacks obtained such work because they accepted the back-breaking labor required in moving crossties, bridge timbers, and T-iron rails. Thus the members of the section crew who maintained the stretch of Seaboard tracks running through Bladenboro were all black, except for the white foreman. Others took jobs digging ditches and stumps, doing the clean-up and heavy work in the larger stores (such as the Bridger Corporation Store), being the handyman at the Seaboard's depot, laboring at the many sawmills in the area, barning tobacco, picking cotton, and so on. Many blacks worked on the farms as sharecroppers or tenant farmers, and some were small landowners who farmed solely for themselves. With no access to the "inside" jobs in the Bladenboro Cotton Mills--even when these infrequently became available--blacks took whatever work they could find. The ones who lived in this day-to-day, hand-to-mouth fashion were at the very bottom of the prevailing social structure. Of course, during the thirties they had plenty of white company in dire circumstances. What separated whites and blacks with identical economic problems was race.

Within the black community, there was also a division based on factors other than education and occupations. Blacks lived both in and around Bladenboro. They clustered east of town in a section referred to as the "quarters"; however, as noted above, some whites also lived there, even relatives (for example, Aunt Clara and Uncle D[aniel] Tyler) and Grover Pait, a prominent businessman who operated a small trucking firm. Another black settlement lay north of town on the Elizabethtown road (NC 242) and another, also north of town, on the Butler Mill road. The residents there were small property holders and included the more "respectable" blacks--the teachers, the craftsmen and those who were perceived to be more "ambitious." And west of town about two miles beyond the Bladenboro Cotton Mills on NC 211 was another thriving black settlement called Richardson. It was there that Sofa Hester, our family's washerwoman, lived. Generally, the home sites and houses--at least the exteriors--reflected the status of the owners. The school principal lived in a nice brick house directly east of town not distant from Spaulding-Monroe school, which he directed, while those who worked at common labor lived more often than not--like many whites at the time--in dilapidated housing, some of it nearly unfit for human habitation. Within the black community, therefore, there was great diversity.

Occasionally, a talented black would break out of the quagmire that stifled his life and head to the North, the West or somewhere else. Infrequently, news circulated that some "colored" person's son or daughter, after having graduated from college, was doing well in some distant place like Baltimore or New York. Or, one might hear of a black like Pate Willis whose daughters all obtained college educations. But as a general rule, black children growing up in the thirties in Bladenboro were entrapped like the children of white cotton mill families. Although a few escaped into richer and fuller lives, the number doing so was very few.

From the perspective of local, contemporary blacks, these observations about their status may seem overly simplistic, even inaccurate. For no one other than blacks who suffered the personal hurts, insults, and indignities of racial discrimination can truly portray their status as it was in those difficult times. The same was true of the mill people who, although white, suffered their own form of discrimination. Because they were white, their status was higher than that of blacks in the local social order--but, not much higher. While blacks suffered racial slurs and other forms of discrimination, mill people endured occupational slurs which indicated the low esteem in which they were held by many in the community. Terms like "lint heads" and "cotton heads" may not have generated the same level of emotional response among them as "n-----" provoked among blacks, but the mill hands understood the implications of the terms. They knew that apart from their work as (for example, as doffers and spinners) they had no respectable status in the community.

Although many cotton mill hands were the offsprings of mill-working parents, in the thirties most of them had been drawn from the surrounding countryside in a process similar to that used in recruiting my Grandfather Asie Suggs and his large family of eight children (five sons and three daughters) from their Brunswick County farm. Sometime during the early twenties Arthur, the oldest son, found a job in the mills of nearby East Lumberton. A second son, Noah, soon followed. Shortly thereafter the entire family left the farm when a mill superintendent offered jobs to all old enough to work, a company house for the family, and a truck to move household belongings without cost to the mill village. My father, who was then eleven, and his older, unemployed brothers and sisters quickly had jobs "learning" to doff and spin at three cents per hour.

In a similar fashion, my maternal great grandparents, Daniel and Exie Hester, reared ten children (five sons and five daughters) who, with the exception of Blaine and Fannie, spent most of their working lives in the Bladenboro Cotton Mills or the mills of nearby Lumberton, St. Pauls, or Rockingham. And their brood of grandchildren began to enter the mills in the late thirties. In such a manner, the mills fleshed out their labor force with the sturdy members of farm families who were accustomed to long hours at hard labor. Without skills and formal education, they generally viewed their movement into the mill villages as a step up in their standard of living.

As in the case of blacks, there was an unfortunate tendency among "outsiders" to see rank-and-file mill hands as a monolithic mass of ignoramuses and to refer to them as "lint heads" or worse. In the Southern cotton mills of the thirties and forties, workers often worked in an dangerous ocean of lint. As a boy I recall seeing my black-haired father and other workers leaving the mills with their heads white with lint. For some reason, outsiders seemed to enjoy applying a derogatory term like "lint heads" and "cotton heads" to textile workers who lived on the mill villages or mill "hills" as the villages were locally called. For example, in Bladenboro most workers lived either on the "old mill hill" or the "new mill hill." Such derogatory terms suggested that village life had nothing to commend it, that only the most immoral and meanest sort of people lived there. The aspersions implied that residence in the villages was a stigma that "respectable" people ought to avoid at all costs. Users of such terms viewed the worst features of village life as typical; they credited all village dwellers with the outrageous behavior and misdeeds of a few. Outsiders "looked down" on mill people and rarely made distinctions among them. They lumped them all together into one homogenous mass while focusing on the worst elements in the mill community.

As a result, many of the "respectable" families in town and country discouraged their children from associating with mill children, or, "mill brats" as they were sometimes disparagingly called, because they feared a social contamination. Such associations, however, were unavoidable in Bladenboro's large consolidated school, which then was reported to be the largest such school in the state. To counter the negative impact of this undesirable association, non-mill parents often attempted to reduce their children's out-of-school social contacts with children of mill workers, especially in sensitive relationships like dating, and so on. This strategy, howcvcr, was not always successful. Young people from the mill villages, town and country did occasionally socialize, but too frequently young women from mill families discovered that a serious relationship rarely developed from their contacts with young males from outside the villages. They sometimes found themselves "used" and dropped. And young men from the village were not likely to be invited into the homes of town residents for social purposes.

Mill residents responded principally in two ways to the social disdain of outsiders. They accepted it, coalesced into a tighter community for self protection, and confined most of their relationships with people whose lives revolved around the mills. They created a tightly knit, self-contained world that seemingly took pride in fulfilling the image held by non-mill residents. Others reacted differently. An awareness of the disdain of outsiders caused many mill residents to strive vigorously to move off the villages, to establish residence anywhere but on the "hills." They wished to avoid the stigma that resulted from their living there. Many longed to acquire a small farm, to own a home, or to keep their children from working in the mills. For some, therefore, escaping from the village became a passionate goal. Many tried to leave and failed because of the difficult times. Others persisted until they successfully extricated themselves from the villages but not necessarily from the mill culture.

My parents, together with a few of their relatives and friends, were in this latter category. The process of escaping was never easy. My parents started their married lives living on the "old mill hill," where I was born, but before they could permanently established themselves elsewhere, circumstances forced them to return to the "hill." They moved off again and were forced to return. This happened several times. I don't think that their yo-yo-like movements were unusual for those with a strong yearning and determination to dissociate themselves from village life. This struggle to leave, for whatever reason, made such members of the mill community seem "different" from the majority who seemingly accepted their lot and were content to live indefinitely in company housing controlled entirely by the mill owners. The former's apparent rejection of village life often produced tension with the majority resident who assumed that those leaving or trying to leave thought themselves to be "better" than those who stayed, or, "too good" to remain in the community.

Outsiders who lumped all mill families together often failed to notice the sacrificial efforts made by many workers to own their homes and "pea patches." For example, a man like LeRoy Brown, who worked years in the Bladenboro Cotton Mills, owned a frame house and a small acreage several miles from the mills. He preferred to live some distance from his work and to commute to his work by car, the ownership of which also distinguished him from most mill hands because few of them owned automobiles. Brown was thus not a typical mill hand content to live on the village in company-owned housing. He was different in his aspirations.

Although most workers depended entirely on the mills for their livelihood, like Brown some did not. More often than not, they lived off the villages and combined their mill jobs with other occupations, such as farming. Some workers owned small patch farms that allowed them to combine farming and mill work without closely identifying with the mill culture. Doing so was not easy, but the thirties were unusual times that often demanded extra effort to survive. Besides, the mills were often on "short time" because of "short orders," with the work being divided among the labor force. Once in the late thirties, my father and Uncle Daniel "D" Tyler sharecropped the Latt Edwards' farm, they providing the labor and Bill Cain, a small store owner and former mill hand, paying the farm rental and initial costs of seed and tobacco plants. Their farming venture was a disaster for nothing went right. And my Uncle Major Suggs, who had acquired a small acreage, and his wife Idus successfully combined work in the mills with farming. For many mill hands who had entered the mills from the farms, there remained a strong nostalgic longing for the land, especially in the spring when plowing and planting were underway throughout the area. My father was like that. Spring always reawakened his craving to own a farm and to have the independence that he identified with it. The mill hands who owned land or who aspired to land ownership and refused to accept the permanence of their lives in the mills were also "different" from the bulk of the workers.

The same was true for others who either combined their mill jobs with other work or broke away entirely while their wives continued as mill hands. For example Bud Edwards spent most of his younger days in the mills, but in mid-life set up a small store near the "old mill hill" and, with his wife Magdalene continuing her job in the "old" mill, managed a successful small business that catered to his former fellow workers. And Graham Pait, an eccentric bachelor known for his sharp tongue, intelligence and wit, set up a small store on Pine Ridge not far from the "new" mill west of town while continuing to work there. Cecil Bennett, who worked for years in the mills, established a successful small business also near the "new" mill, managing it while his wife Flora continued on as a mill hand. And Mollie Cain remained in the mill until the store which she and her husband Bill operated on Highway 211 was successful enough for her to quit. Although small time, these working-class entrepreneurs were obviously a cut above the majority of mill employees in their view of the possible.

Furthermore, there was an occasional mill hand who felt the "call" to preach and did so, combining religious responsibilities with mill work. Gaston Hester was such a man. For much of his early career as a minister, he worked in the mills, preached on Sundays, and married and buried the members of his congregation when called upon. He eventually became a full-time minister at the West Bladenboro Baptist and other churches. And there was Holland Hughes who worked as a mill hand and preached for Holiness churches for many, many years. He never reached a point in his ministry when it was possible to surrender his job in the mills. Reverend H. C. Adcox, a Free Will Baptist minister, also worked for awhile in the "old" mill before age made that impractical. And Julian Smith, another "Holiness" evangelist, combined mill work with preaching. The wives of these men who heeded the "call" were also mill hands who supported the second careers of their husbands. Without that backing, their religious work would not have been possible. The activities of these men, who also eventually moved off the villages, illustrated the diversity among the workers.

There was also a natural division among the mill hands based on the jobs they held within the mills. Without a doubt, the lowest job that one could hold was that of sweeper. It was a dirty, filthy job that no worker really wanted unless there was no other option. With a wide broom especially designed to trap the lint that constantly fell, the sweeper's job was to periodically clean the hardwood aisles between the machines. What made his job unusually distasteful was the widespread habit among the workers and their bosses of dipping snuff or chewing tobacco and spitting huge quantities of "juice" around the support beams of the mill, the water fountain, and the legs of the machines. Thus when sweeping up the lint, the sweeper also collected the sputum and the discarded "wads" of dozens of tobacco users, thereby placing himself at risk to one of the most feared diseases of the day--tuberculosis. Almost anyone entering the mill for the first time might be stuck with this dangerous job. This was an "inside" job which even blacks were not privileged to hold until after World War II. Ironically, racial discrimination kept them "outside" in the yard where the air was reasonably clean and fresh.

Probably the most prestigious job in the mill was that of machinist or electrician. During the early forties, the Kinlaw brothers had a lock on the machinist positions in the Bladenboro Cotton Mills. Charley and Tally Kinlaw worked in a "shop" adjacent to an old furnace room. The shop was located above the elevated tracks parallel to the Old Mill from which coal was once dropped from hopper cars to feed the furnaces. The atmosphere in the machine shop was very different from that in the mills. In the summertime the windows were usually open and, if one went inside, the pleasant hum of lathes turning and grinding out gears and other parts for the textile machinery, which needed constant repair, was interrupted only by the occasional high-pitched whirring of a banding machine turning out all-purpose bands. The noise of lathes and drills, the oily odor of the lumbering machines, the sight of buckets of gears and steel filings, and the extraordinary skill with which the men adjusted the machines and used their measuring instruments--all were fascinating to the senses. These were no ordinary workers. Their work seemed to be enormously complicated, requiring a level of skill much beyond that of spinners, doffers and others in the mills. This was evident, too, in the deference that other workers showed the Kinlaws who had mastered their mysterious craft. Electricians, like Bill Hester, also fell into this same category. Somewhere between the machinists/electricians and the sweepers lay all the other workers, including minor supervisory personnel like section-hands and fixers. There was clearly a pecking order in the mills based on skills and jobs.

Of course, there were also differences based on the religion which many of the workers professed and practiced. With a few exceptions, they attended the churches within a radius of a mile around the mills. Their denominations included the Missionary Baptist (Southern Baptist), the Free Will Baptist, the Fire Baptized Holiness, the Church of God, and others. There wasn't a great difference between these bodies except in religious fervor. All were fundamentalist, Protestant churches that were filled with dirt-poor people. Nevertheless, there was enough difference to make for much lively discussions among the religious minded throughout the work week. I suppose that there were more similarities than differences, but many workers took great pride in displaying their religious distinctiveness. Some emphasized outward appearances, for example, refusing to wear make-up, jewelry or adornments of any kind. Others stressed the fervor of their religious experience, for example, pointing to their state of "holiness" in their shouting, talking in tongues, and faith healing. Others demonstrated their religious commitment by refraining from card playing, swearing, movies, dancing, and smoking. These differences, although outwardly superficial, were very important to devout mill hands, and they were the subject of endless conversations at work. Within the mill community religion really made a difference in determining the behavior of believers. It helped to separate them from those ne'er-do-wells who largely determined the "outside" perceptions of the mill people. Paradoxically, it drew them together while distinguishing them from each other.

Like the blacks, the mill people were subjected to their own forms of discrimination in the larger community. Perhaps the most damaged were their children who were informally taught in dozens of ways that they were inferior because their parents worked in the cotton mills, that they were fated to do the same, and that they were foolish to aspire to new horizons. When believed, these negative views became self-fulfilling. Perhaps without meaning to be, the public schools became the principal tool whereby this was done. As a grade school student this realization came to me when my mother visited my school and demanded that I be returned to the class of Miss Altie Stone who was recognized as being the "best" third grade teacher in the elementary school. How did my mother know that Miss Stone was the "best" teacher? For her the question was easy to answer. Enrolled in Miss Stone's class was every third-grade child of the mill-owning families living on Front Street. My prior removal from Miss Stone's class had offended her, too, because I had been a member of the group since the first grade. Because my grades were high, she assumed that there were other reasons for my transfer to the "B" section of the third grade. She was certain that it resulted from my father's work in the mills. She was determined that I remain in the "top" track. As a result of her efforts, I remained there.

There were other indications in the schools that the children of mill folk were held in low esteem. It was the custom for each elementary class to have a "chapel" program sometime during the year, or, a class might be asked to prepare a skit or program for a session of the local PTA. The children chosen for the lead roles in these performances were invariably from families living on Front Street or, occasionally, the farms. Bright youngsters from the mill villages quickly learned the score and, if fortunate enough to reach high school, they simply made no effort to secure prominent places in school activities.

The frequent result was intense frustration and an undermining of self-confidence and self-worth for the mill children, and for the others a distorted sense of their own importance and abilities. As a freshman in high school, I overheard the daughter of a mill hand shouting hysterically at a teacher because she believed that the teacher had treated her unfairly solely because she lived on the "old mill hill." Was the teacher guilty of the charge? Who knows? But there was no doubt in the student's mind that where she lived made a difference in how her teacher perceived and treated her. Furthermore, at one time corporal punishment was fairly common in the public schools. Rumors often circulated among the mill people that the corporal punishment meted out to their children was unduly severe as compared to others. The stories, often unfounded, fed on such incidents as the punishment of Ozell Hester who once returned home from school with belt marks on his back. His mill-working parents were convinced that school officials would not have dared to belt-whip a child living on Front Street or the farm. Because of these episodes and the reaction of their parents, children of mill hands sensed the gulf separating them from the rest of the community. Their recognition originated not in the formal instructions of the schools but perhaps in the unconscious subtleties of class expressed in different treatment. That awareness sometime became explosive.

Shortly after James Shipman, son of mill workers, returned from the military service following World War II, he opened a hamburger stand outside Butters, which is located several miles west of Bladenboro. One evening, a very close friend of mine who was the son of mill hands, became embroiled in an argument with another friend who was the son of a mill owner, outside Shipman's business. I shall never forget the bitterness of the former when he told the latter that he longed to see the day when the entire membership of the mill-owning clan would starve. He expressed the hope that all of them would find it necessary to push peanuts up Front Street with their noses while begging for food. Part of this vehemence, of course, was boyish hoopla. But it occurred to me that what I was hearing was chronic frustration approaching an extraordinary level of bitterness. How many other children of mill workers felt this way?--even temporarily? No one will ever know. However, I don't think that he was alone in his bitterness and hostility toward the mill owners, most of whom were fine and decent people.

Did public school teachers *deliberately* cultivate class awareness among their students? I have never thought so. But there is no question that they *informally* taught attitudes which generated a sense of class among children of different social and economic backgrounds. Perhaps for them it was a matter of survival. The times were hard and teaching positions were scarce in the thirties. Under the circumstances, favoritism to the children of Front Streeters made good sense in helping to insure next year's contract. Perhaps it was nothing more than a natural identification with the children of people like themselves. For the most part, their social life, such as it was, was the same as that of Front Streeters in whose homes they sometimes boarded. Furthermore, most of them attended the First Baptist Church on Front Street which, in the minds of the mill people, was the church of the mill owners.

Even so, it was extremely unlikely that teachers of that era would have socialized with mill people with whom they had little in common. Besides, such social contacts would have been discouraged by the local school committee, that is, if the socializing had become known. Nevertheless, the teachers in the Bladenboro elementary schools were extremely competent. Thanks to my mother, I was taught by the "best" teachers in the system, and thanks to her each of my teachers quickly knew that she would accept nothing less than equal treatment for her son. In this stand she was supported by my father who had the good sense to marry a strong-willed woman who considered herself and her family "no better than but just as good as anybody." The result was that I never developed the sense that I was discriminated against because my father worked in the Bladenboro Cotton Mills. On the contrary, I had good rapport with my teachers who treated me neither better nor worse than the most favored students in the school.

Higher than the mill people and the blacks in the social structure of Bladenboro were the white farmers who lived within a radius of five to ten miles of town. Many of them enjoyed a standard of living no better than the mill people. Nevertheless, the farmers who eked out a living on their own land generally possessed a status denied to the workers. Owning land, even a small patch farm of ten or fifteen acres, frequently conferred a measure of community respect. There were exceptions of course, to this general rule. For example, one small, landowning farmer whom I knew lived with his family in a dilapidated shack with a dirt floor located southeast of town toward Whiteville in a section called "Hog Wallow" because of the frequent flooding. He barely survived economically. Land ownership failed to bring him the respect that it customarily brought, perhaps because of his lifestyle. A rumor circulated that once A. A. White, the superintendent of the local school, visited the this man's home to investigate his children's absence from the classroom. According to the rumor, which was undoubtedly exaggerated, as White went in through the front door hogs ran out the back door. This farmer was clearly not one held in high esteem by the local citizenry, even after being employed later in a respectable town job. He remained an exception to the general rule that land ownership conferred status.

Nonetheless, many landless mill hands like my father longed to own a small farm, believing, even in the face of contradictory evidence, that farming offered an escape from the hard times in the mills. Furthermore, the rhythm of community life was geared to the ebb and flow of seasons rather than to the deadening roar of whirring, textile machinery. Farming was more compatible with this felt rhythm as mill work could never be. Consequently, even mill hands, especially those with farm backgrounds–and there were many–tended to accord the land-owning farmer a deference that reflected their low self-esteem. As my father often noted with envy, a farmer unlike himself, was a free man. He could go to work when he pleased, stop when he pleased, and be master of his own life. He was beholden to no one. Although this perception of farm life was idealized and not entirely true, he nevertheless believed it and so did many of his fellow workers in the mills.

Among the local farmers there were also vast differences. Many of them did not own land. Too many of them worked acreage that they did not own, farming as sharecroppers or as tenants. Their lot during the depression years was extremely difficult. My Uncle Woodrow Edwards (my mother's brother) and his wife Edna farmed as a young couple on land belonging to Dr. Dewey Herbert Bridger. Woodrow was an excellent tobacco farmer. But as children multiplied, his life was gradually consumed farming Bridger's land located southeast of town near the Columbus County line. The house that he and his family were provided was woefully inadequate in space, facilities, and so on. Houses on the mill villages were far superior to the dwelling where this hard-working family struggled to exist. The children grew up and Woodrow and Edna grew old together in this house without much ever being done to improve it before the children began to disperse. Respectable and hard-working, they nevertheless were low in status in the regional social structure because they were tenant farmers. There were many like them who lived in similar circumstances.

Superior in status to the tenants and sharecroppers were the numerous landowning farmers. They tended to cluster in family networks around the town in sections that often bore their name or that of a nearby church where they attended services. South of town toward Evergreen was Lennon's Crossroads, a community so named because of the number of Lennons who lived there. Central to its life was the Lennon's Crossroads Baptist Church which was also attended by a number of farm families living in the area (for example, the Clyde Evanses and the George Kellys). If one traveled north from Bladenboro toward Dublin, one encountered other farm-family networks--the Britts, the Doves, the Singletarys, the Bryants, and the Paits. Or, if one moved north over the Elizabethtown road toward Sandy Grove Church, one found that area populated by the Storms, the Guytons, and the Whites. And the region north toward Tarheel contained networks of Hickmans and Brissons. South of town on the Whiteville road were the Wards and Edwards, and around the Mt. Calvary Free Will Baptist Church were numerous Browns and Ransoms. While blacks clustered together in their own communities because of racial discrimination and the majority of mill hands resided in the villages to be near their work, the clustering of the small, landowning farmers around Bladenboro seemed to be largely determined by family linkage. However, this homing into family networks was not unique to the farm people. Family ties were also extremely important in attracting entire families into the mills, especially if a family member was in a position to hire.

The Clyde Evans family was typical of this class of respectable, landowning farmers. Living off the meager returns from tobacco, corn and peanuts raised on a small acreage situated in the Lennon's Crossroads section south of town, Evans and his wife produced a family of healthy sons and daughters who began moving lockstep through the public schools. In the late thirties and forties, it seemed that an Evans graduated from Bladenboro High School each year and moved on to a life off the farm, usually into a career that involved a college education. In addition to being a successful farmer, Evans served as a school committeeman. Both he and his wife were perceived as pillars of their community. The high esteem in which they were held rubbed off on their vivacious, talented children who, unlike many of the youngsters from the mill villages, never had cause to question their acceptance and status in the schools or the general community. Assured and self-confident, they were involved in athletics and all school activities ranging from the Beta Club to school bus drivers. They enjoyed an easy relationship with the children of the Front Street families who seemed to accept them readily.

Not all farm children, however, had such an assured status. North of town toward Dublin was a large settlement of Paits whose offsprings were conspicuous in the school classes of the early forties. Like the Evans, the Paits were hard-working, respectable, and landowning, but their children were never accorded the same deference from fellow students and teachers as that shown to the Evans. To some extent, of course, this difference in treatment lay in contrasting personalities. Even so, I cannot recall an incident in which a farm child clashed with a teacher over alleged discrimination because of their parents' occupation. Generally, their treatment in the school reflected the respected and majority status of their parents. But even among the small, landowning farmers there were wide differences which were reflected in the peer relationships of their children.

Resting at the very top of the social structure were the Front Street families whose position was rarely challenged. Composing this diverse group were the mill owners, a small number of professionals, a variety of small shop owners, several small-time entrepreneurs, and store clerks and mechanics. Within this stratum there was also great diversity of status based on property ownership, education, family, and so on. At the bottom were the clerks who worked in the ten or twelve businesses that made up the town. Some of these individuals spent most of their working lives in the same mercantile establishment. The largest store was the Bridger Corporation that catered primarily to the area farmers and less so to the mill workers. Men like Graham Wilson, Dewey Guyton, and Bernard Ward worked there until their retirement or death. The same was true of Evelyn Thompson who, prior to becoming a clerk, had helped run a kindergarten on the "old mill village." And across the street in the Bridger Drug Store worked C. A. Shaw, a man whose working life was mostly spent there. West on NC 211 toward Lumberton was the "company store" of the Bladenboro Cotton Mills managed by Emmett Guyton who worked there as long as I can remember. In some respect, these people were more than simply clerks because each of them exercised managerial roles in their firms. Furthermore, some individuals in this subgroup attained the highest reputation within the community. For example, when Graham Wilson died of cancer in the mid-forties, most businesses shut down during his funeral and burial out of respect for the man. But the average behind-the-counter clerk, men like "Streety" Benton who worked in the meat market at the Bridger Corporation, led unremarked and undistinguished lives.

A notch up were the small shop owners who owned and operated barber shops, groceries, filling stations, restaurants, pool halls, and "department" stores. Azzie Hardin and Charley Bell Ward operated barber shops for years, with Ward clipping hair for more than fifty years in the same location. Allie Page with her husband Moseley and stepchildren persisted in trying to make a go of restaurants which on Sundays catered to the after-church crowd drawn principally from Front Street First Baptist Church of Bladenboro. And there was Ed Lewis who operated a furniture store and a funeral business. For awhile, Lewis kept his stock of caskets upstairs above his store near the Bank of Bladenboro before moving his operations to another part of town. Oz Hester ran a bicycle and repair shop; D. H. Russ operated a small grocery; J. V. Vaught owned the Cash Store; M. Nance operated a fish and hamburger stand next to Vaught's store; Lizzie Dunn beautified the ladies at her beauty parlor; Woody Hilburn managed the Seaboard Railway depot; Pelo Lockamy ran a pool room; W. G. Fuzzell owned the Lyric Theatre that later became the Wonet; Jodie Bennett ran a cleaning establishment; William "Bill" Hussey operated a grocery and, after the war, a builders' supply business. The Searles family ran a "five and dime." Truett Freeman ran a jewelry store. And Henry White owned and operated a livery stable, selling horses and mules. Small businesses could also be found outside the town limits. West on NC 211, for example, were such places as Smithy Edwards' hamburger emporium, the Eagle Eye (at one time a very rowdy place), Albert Thompson's store and filling station, Asie Hardin's filling station, and Caz Deaver's store. The interesting thing about these proprietors was the vast differences in education, success, and so on. Caz Deaver, for example, was completely illiterate, being unable to read or write. However, he developed his own pictographic system of accounting for recording the charges of his customers.

Among the Front Streeters were several small-time entrepreneurs. West of town on NC 211, Carey Dowless operated a trucking firm consisting of several tractor-trailers. He was a frequent carrier for the Bladenboro Cotton Mills. And east of town, Grover Pait owned a small trucking firm that sent trucks with hogsheads of tobacco, textiles, and other products to distant places. Although never conspicuous in community affairs, Dowless and Pait were nevertheless "different" by virtue of their business activities. Operating successful trucking firms in a small, farming and mill town required intelligence, imagination and, of course, the willingness to assume considerable financial risks.

Although few in numbers, the professionals in Bladenboro were essential to the life of the community. Lloyd Elkins, a graduate of Duke University Law School, was the only lawyer in town. He did not have a thriving practice. Although brilliant, most of Elkins' work consisted of routine legal matters, such as the preparation of deeds and conveyances, because he refused to serve as a trial lawyer. The town was fortunate to have two physicians--Dr. S. S. Hutchinson and Dr. Dewey H. Bridger–and one dentist, a Dr. Nance whose office was above the Bank of Bladenboro. There was no professional pharmacist until after World War II when one was employed by Dr. Hutchinson. Composing the bulk of the professionals were the public school teachers, most of whom were females with college degrees. They were a seasoned corps characterized by toughness and dedication, at least until World War II ravaged their ranks. Boarding with families like the W. G. Fussells on Front Street and the Woody Hilburns on Back Street, they contributed much to the cohesion and self-assurance among the Front Streeters.

Topping the social structure was the network of Bridger families who owned not only the cotton mills but nearly all the important community enterprises. Their widespread ownership of property, their control over practically all economic activity, and their general domination of life made them the overlords of the town. In the postwar years, it was rumored that they occasionally used their power to deny access to new businesses which might challenge their dominance by competing with their mills and other family ventures. Although the Bladenboro Cotton

Mills (Joe Bridger), the Bridger Corporation (Livingston Bridger), the Bank of Bladenboro (Levy Bridger), the Bridger Drugstore (Dr. Dewey H. Bridger), and the Bridger Motor Company (James A. Bridger) were the major enterprises owned by the Bridgers, their interests were far more extensive. For example, most of the small merchants noted above rented space for their groceries, barber shops, and so on from one Bridger or another. They also owned substantial nearby farmlands on which they placed tenants and sharecroppers. By controlling local access to jobs in the mills, bank credit, farming necessities (for example, fertilizers and equipment), business opportunities, and rental properties, they made their presence pervasive.

The status of the Bridgers was evidenced in their substantial homes which faced each other across Front Street, the "Street of Beautiful Homes." At a time when practically no one in the area enrolled at colleges and universities because of hard times and the expense, the sons of prominent Bridgers went off to military academies or prep schools for their senior year in high school, to be followed by enrollment at schools like Wake Forest, North Carolina State, and the University of North Carolina. Their daughters enrolled at Woman's College at Greensboro, Meredith, Queens, and Peace. Their summers were often spent at family cottages located at Carolina, Wrightsville, and other Carolina beaches. In looking at class pictures taken during the thirties, with a few exceptions it is possible to pick out their children by the quality of the clothes they wore. But perhaps most important, their status was evidenced by the deference which others paid to the Bridger clan. When Joe Bridger, president of the Bladenboro Cotton Mills, went into Charley Bell Ward's barber shop for a haircut and shave, waiting customers jovially allowed tobacco-chewing "Mr. Joe" to have the first available chair. As already noted, their children were always up front in school activities. And the influence of the Bridger families was statewide. James Albert Bridger, owner of the Bridger Motor Company, was a state representative and later had sufficient political clout to be named to the important State Highway Commission in the mid-forties. His appointment tremendously benefitted Bladen Countians who soon had all their rural roads paved. Because of the contributions to Wake Forest University, the Dr. Dewey H. Bridger family held influential positions on governing bodies of that school.

Privileged and advantaged, the Bridgers sat serenely and unchallenged atop local society until World War II and the G.I. Bill thrust numerous opportunities for travel, self-discovery and education upon hundreds of former service men and women who never dreamed that they would have them. Nevertheless, all things considered, the Bridgers were a distinguished family who contributed greatly to the economic development of the town and the region. For example, for many years their Bladenboro Cotton Mills were the largest employer in Bladen County. If they ever questioned the rightness of their status, it went unnoticed. They accepted their dominance and good fortune, seemingly unaware that it often generated undertows of anger among some of the less fortunate in the community.

Chapter 2

Black Faces Among White Faces

Although Southern society was formally segregated in the thirties and forties, there were nonetheless frequent, informal contacts between blacks and whites in Bladenboro that tended to ameliorate the natural antagonism that legal segregation of the races inevitably produced. These informal contacts, occurring in a variety of ways and situations, thus served to strengthen positive relationships between individual blacks and whites that made life in this small Southern town more tolerable and humane for all. In effect, they softened the harshness of a segregated system and inexorably caused some individuals to disregard or to minimize color in their personal relationships and to relate to one another as people. Nevertheless, the pernicious effects of the system hovered always near the surface in such biracial relationships, a poisonous presence waiting to assert itself.

Evidence of segregation abounded. The Bladenboro Public Schools, reported to be the largest consolidated system in the state during the thirties, enrolled its students separately. Blacks attended their own Spaulding-Monroe School, located on the east side of town in what was then derisively called the "Quarters." Whites rode school busses past the black school en route to class, while blacks rode busses past the white school en route to their own. There were no extra-curricular, sports or interscholastic contacts of any kind between the student bodies. The professional staffs were also segregated and rarely, if ever, met with each other in workshops, in meetings to share problems, and so on. Even the professional teacher organizations were separate and never had formal, common meetings.

Furthermore, the Bladenboro Cotton Mills, the major employer in town, also segregated its workforce. Although the company employed a few black males, it was careful to use them on jobs that necessitated minimal contacts with white workers. It did not hire black women, even though a major percentage of its workforce was composed of females. Until after World War II, blacks worked only on the outside, leaving even the dirtiest and filthiest industrial jobs inside the mills, such as sweeper, to whites. Blacks were employed principally in the yards and in the cotton warehouses to move the heavy bales of cotton that flowed there in an endless stream to feed the mills. They also worked an assortment of odd jobs--digging and filling holes for the outdoor privies on the all-white mill villages, cleaning and disinfecting the inside toilets of the mills, shoveling coal into the hugh furnaces of the boiler room, doing yard work around the homes of the mill owners, and so on. Although few in numbers, blacks were highly visible in the mill yards. A visitor there was certain to see them at work under Jasper V. Pittman, a stocky, nearly bald supervisor who wore glasses, who managed the cotton inventories and the warehouses. In my years of observing the mills, I recall only one black performing an inside-the-mill job, that is, a job operating machines. In the early fifties, I found one working in the picker room of the company's new mill, a workplace so full of lint that it was difficult to breathe. Prior to World War II, blacks worked the outside jobs which, ironically, provided them with a hidden benefit denied to white workers--that is, less opportunity to contract byssinosis or brown lung disease, commonly called "mill fever."

Religious denominations also bowed to the imposition of legal segregation. Like the schools and the cotton mills, churches in and around Bladenboro were separated according to race. (There were also religious and cultural differences which further divided the white churches, about which more later.) Two churches served the black community east of town. Located near Spaulding-Monroe School, the AME Church drew worshippers from the north and east of town, as did the larger Baptist Church. Another church, the Brown Branch Church, was situated about two miles west on Highway 211 toward Richardson, a thriving, black settlement. These three were among the dozen or more churches found within a radius of five miles from Bladenboro. If there was any linkage between the black and white churches to further their Christian purposes, it was not evident in co-operative programs, ministerial associations, or congregational associations. It was rare for these bodies to be mutually supportive, whatever the cause. In my family's church (White Oak Free Will Baptist Church), I recall only one service in which blacks were present. One Sunday evening, a black choral group rendered a program of sacred music and was well received by the few members of the congregation in attendance.

Other obvious forms of segregation existed. At the insistence of the living, the separation that divided blacks and whites in life persisted into death. With a few exceptions, most cemeteries were located on church property, although high water tables prevented burials near a few churches. This invariably meant that the deceased was buried with his own kind--if white with whites, if black with blacks. Family graveyards not owned by churches also tended to be black or white, the pull of race remaining strong among the descendants of the dead. For example, local blacks buried their dead in a cemetery less than a mile north of town on the Elizabethtown road, or in an obscure plots such as that near the Latt Edwards family cemetery off the Butler Mill road. Whites buried theirs in the Bridger Cemetery (now known as Pine Crest) about a mile south of town near the Bladenboro Public Schools, or the Mill Cemetery across Highway 211 from the New Mill. Other cemeteries were located at various churches--Oak Grove, Sandy Grove, Mount Calvary, Zion Hill, Lennon's Crossroads, and others. Occasionally, the two races would be found in the same cemetery, but in different sections. This practice was followed by the caretakers of the Singletary Cemetery at Butters, a former lumber camp situated about four miles west of town on the edge of the Big Swamp near the Robeson County line.

Furthermore, the passenger cars of the Seaboard Railroad, which each day ran an eastbound and westbound train through the town, were segregated, one car for blacks and one for whites. As a child living in the old Hales house near the local depot, I often sat in the gazebo near the tracks and watched black and white faces staring out from separate cars. The depot was also segregated. It had separate black and white waiting rooms. W. G. Fussell's Lyric Theatre and its successor, the Wonet, were also segregated, the whites sitting in the downstairs auditorium and the blacks occupying the balcony for the movies. Except for "kitchen help," the town's cafes were segregated. I never saw a black, not even a professional black, eating in a local cafe. And, of course, the clerks in the stores were all white. Blacks were sometimes used as handymen to move stock and sweep the floors. No blacks belonged to the local Boy Scout Troop 72, which was sponsored by a white Rotary Club and led by white leaders. In short, private and public institutions in Bladenboro were organized around the principle of segregation, just as was the rest of the state and the South.

Under such circumstances, it would seem that opportunities for positive relationships between blacks and whites were nil. However, this was not the case because, in spite of the official segregation that characterized life in Bladenboro and the South, circumstances forced the two races to co-mingle, to discover each other, and to work out a liveable, if not wholly ideal accommodation. In many instances, individuals developed genuine respect and affection for each other. For example, both my father and I liked and enormously respected Carl Singletary, a black man who for awhile cleaned and dressed fish at Taylor's Grocery store and later Blanco Duvall's store and did various jobs for other stores.

Because of character, force of personality or whatever, some blacks became accepted "institutions" in the community. Such a man was "Shorty," a dwarf who had found favor with tobacco-chewing Joe Bridger, president of the Bladenboro Cotton Mills. "Shorty" was a glaring exception to the discrimination against blacks who worked for the cotton mills because he held a job that was considered a "white man's job." In addition to keeping up the grounds around Bridger's shingled mansion on Front Street, he worked with Corbett Hester, a white man, as week-end watchman at the mills. With a large clock suspended on a leather strap slung across his shoulder, "Shorty" made his rounds, wobbling his small stature forward from side to side on very short legs.

He was an effective watchman. An unusually black black man who immediately attracted attention because of his shortness and his ready smile, he was known to have the ear of Bridger and thus carried an aura of authority that belied his size and color. He also had an unusual amount of compassion and common sense. One Sunday afternoon, he came upon a group of mill youngsters, including me, who were throwing chunks of coal and "clinkers" through the window panes of the boiler room of the company's Old Mill. His shout caused the older boys to scatter, leaving me and several of the youngest to face the music. Speaking sternly, he warned us never to break windows again and then sent us scurrying home. However, this did not end the matter. "Shorty" knew my father and spoke to him privately about what his son had done, rather than make an issue of the incident that could have been damaging not only to me but my father. Needless to say, I did not break any more mill windows, but I did remember his kindness. Years later, I saw him display that inherent kindness again. One of R. C. Bridger's (Joe Bridger's successor as president of the Bladenboro Cotton Mills) very young sons had wandered from home across several streets and the Seaboard Railway tracks into the downtown area clothed in something that resembled a diaper. "Shorty," who was leaning against a power pole in front of the Bridger Drugstore, took the child by the hand and wobbled off toward the boy's home--a very short black man and a very young white child linked by kindness and trust. Such a scene was a palliative to racial antagonism caused by segregation.

By the quality of their lives other blacks helped to ameliorate the destructive effects of segregation upon the white mind, especially the minds of children. In the thirties, the white elementary school, a large two-storied building, was heated by steam produced by a coal-fired furnace. Few of the children who attended school in that era can forget the sense of well-being and comfort generated by the ancient radiators that hissed and clanked in the winter as the steam ran through and heated the pipes. And every child in the school knew that the man who was responsible for the warmth radiating throughout the school was a man named Oscar. Oscar was a tall, lean black man who invariably wore bib overalls, and in the winter, a blue denim jacket with copper-colored buttons. It was his job to arrive early, fire the furnace, and keep it going throughout the day by shoveling in the coal when needed. Every child in the school knew Oscar and undoubtedly made the connection between him and the comforting inside heat. A rather solemn man who rarely smiled, Oscar nevertheless was a man who seemed always busy and intent on doing well his many jobs around the school. He was a responsible individual whose work in tending the furnace and providing custodial services was essential in the operation of the school. His was a very familiar face around the building, and this helped to make the presence of black faces among white children as natural as the sun rising. That was perhaps his greatest service. I do not recall a single incident of a white child directing a racial slur toward Oscar or showing him anything but the utmost respect.

The shared experiences of blacks and whites often transcended their separateness and drew them together. During the Great Depression of the thirties, deprivation fell heavily upon the poor of both races. Sharecroppers, tenant farmers, and mill workers in the Bladenboro area--whatever their color--lived constantly on the edge of disaster. Under such circumstances, the ubiquitous harshness of life generated currents of mutual understanding that undermined the walls erected to separate the races. Poor folks--black and white--often reached out to each other in order to endure the hard times.

During my early childhood, the hard times and the sickness of my mother resulted in our family having a very close contact with several black women. Periodically bedridden because of a heart condition, my mother required help in managing her household chores and blacks were employed at one time or another for that purpose. Although quite young, I remember one of these women very well. My father hired Beth (Bet) Purdie to care for me and my mother during one of her illnesses on the days when he was fortunate to have work in the cotton mills. Bet made a greater impression on me than the other women he employed from time to time, partly for the same reasons that she impressed my parents who, for years thereafter, commented favorably about her. They used the same standards in assessing her as they did in judging other people, that is, reliability, honesty, trustworthiness, cleanliness--the latter quality being extremely important to my mother who was unusually fastidious about housekeeping and food preparation. As for myself, I remember her with fondness primarily because she cared for me, it seemed, as she cared for her own children. Bet's work threw our family members into intimate contacts with an admirable black woman whose character positively enhanced our respect for blacks in general. The same was true in the case of Sofa Hester, our black washwoman, whose relationship with the family has been described elsewhere in another book ("My World Is Gone"). Black domestics worked for many of the mill-owning families on Front Street, caring for their children and doing their cooking, washing, ironing and cleaning. The resulting interaction undoubtedly enlightened both races concerning each other.

Like the depression, World War II also produced opportunities that evoked the common humanity in both races and brought them closer together. A case in point was the death and burial of Benjamin Lacy, the son of "Ben" Lacy, a caretaker for the First Baptist Church on Front Street. Benjamin was a serviceman who had been killed in the war. Following a service at his church east of town, his funeral cortege proceeded slowly west on NC 211 to the center of town where it turned north on the Elizabethtown road en route to the nearby black cemetery. In death as in life, Benjamin was to be segregated, his ultimate sacrifice for his country notwithstanding. Because it was Sunday afternoon, many whites, principally young people like myself who traditionally gathered in town to while away the time on the streets or the churchyard of the Presbyterian Church that then sat between the Lyric Theater and the Bank of Bladenboro, quietly watched the solemn procession as it crossed the Bryant Swamp bridge and veered right at the fork in the road toward the cemetery. Spontaneously, a number of us began moving in the same direction, drawn perhaps by the opportunity to observe a military funeral, a rare occurrence in our town even in the midst of war. We arrived as the minister was concluding his grave-side remarks and in time to watch the military ritual.

What followed was an unforgettable scene. Overcome by grief, the mother of the deceased burst forth in soul-wrenching moans. Her anguished cries were accompanied by an uncontrollable weeping and convulsions of the body as she alternately raised her tightly clasped hands to heaven and dropped them to her knees. All the while great beads of sweat and tears rained down from her face. Repeatedly she cried out, "No mo' Ben! Oh Lawd, no mo' Ben!" For the whites in the crowd, the poor woman's mournful, pitiful cry transformed Ben's funeral from an event to enliven a small-town Sunday afternoon to one that evoked great sorrow and compassion for a mother who had lost her son. At least for a moment, mourners and onlookers felt the pain and hurt caused by Benjamin's death, a pain and hurt that transcended race and linked us together in our common humanity. We were united by shared grief. Few eyes remained dry. For me the scene would remain forever a statement of the human condition for all races. For many years afterwards when my father, who was also present for the funeral, and I drove pass the cemetery, one of us would invariably mention Benjamin's funeral and how it affected us.

Although blacks were not employed as clerks in the local stores, some store owners nonetheless used them in support work possibly to attract the business of the many blacks who lived in the area. Furthermore, in some of the larger stores there were disagreeable jobs that were thought particularly suitable for them--"n----- work," that is, jobs involving the lifting of heavy sacks of feed and rolls of hog wire, cleaning and sweeping, working in the stockrooms or warehouses, and so on. But a black who held such a job through long service became clearly identified with the establishment and, I suspect, did indeed attract the trade of many black patrons.

Bill Gillespi was one such man. For several years he worked for the Bridger Corporation, the town's principal mercantile establishment since 1911, until the early forties when William (Bill) and Charles Hussey employed him in their grocery and feed store located in the old Oz Hester building on the corner of NC 211 and NC 410, across from the Bridger Motor Company. Gillespi was an overweight man of medium height who shuffled along at a lumbering pace. His large round, moon-like face, his extremely black skin, and his shifty, white eyes gave him a look of perpetual surprise. His appearance combined with a somber disposition to make him the butt of many practical jokes.

Fellow employees and store patrons--black and white--took pleasure in goosing Gillespi in order to watch his startled reaction and to hear his outcry of "Watch out der!" And a particularly mean trick produced a story that was repeatedly told by many with much laughing--that is, how Bill had inadvertently eaten chicken droppings when he had sneaked what he thought was candy from a display case of the Bridger Corporation store. The "trick" had been designed to end his practice of snitching candy. Afterwards when asked how he liked "Choofies," he pretended to be greatly agitated and to spit out the imaginary droppings--much to the delight of the jokers. Nearly everyone who knew Gillespi had heard the story about the chicken droppings and had good-naturedly asked the question about the "Choofies." Nonetheless he was no buffoon, for the people who kidded and joked with him were usually friends and had no malicious intent.

My close association with Bill Gillespi occurred in the mid-forties when I began working on the weekends for the Hussey brothers, a job which evolved into full-time summer work. Bill was then in his fifties or sixties and was employed on the weekends to help with the increased chores. Most of the business of the week was conducted on Friday afternoon and Saturday when most of the local farmers and mill workers came to town. The Husseys were an ambitious pair and, in spite of the scarcity of consumer goods caused by World War II, they managed to find merchandise to sell. Their warehouse, where Bill worked, was stocked with a variety of supplies--sacks of hog and chicken feed, bales of lespedeza hay, a barrel of black-strap molasses, a chicken coop usually filled with fryers and old hens, rolls of hog and chicken wire when available, a few building supplies--all of which involved Bill in some way or another. If a customer wanted a live hen, it was Bill who retrieved it from the coop; if the customer wanted the hen dressed, it was Bill who performed the task behind the store using makeshift equipment--killing, scalding, plucking and gutting the chicken. It was Bill's job to help load the delivery truck, to draw the molasses, to help load the feed, the wire and the hay. Without ever seeming to rush, he performed these tasks while carrying on endless verbal exchanges with the large numbers of blacks, especially women who seemed to adore him, who traded in the store. Bill and I became friends. For a variety of reasons, I liked him and the feeling was mutual. As Christmas approached in 1945, I promised to sell him a used bike which he wanted as a present for a grandchild. Although the Second World War was over, bikes remained difficult to obtain. We agreed upon a price of ten dollars. But before delivery, a customer in the store heard that I had the bike for sale and tried to purchase it by offering me twenty-five dollars. In spite of my insistence that the bike was already sold, he persisted. Although I needed the extra money, I refused. Unknown to me, Bill, who was working quietly in the back of the warehouse behind sacks of feed, overheard the conversation. After the customer left, he emerged from behind the sacks with a big grin on his shiny moon-face and a ten-dollar bill in his hand. This episode cemented our friendship. I found Bill to be an extremely interesting personality, one of the many who enriched my early years. My wholesome relationship with him greatly influenced my behavior and attitude toward all black people.

Not all blacks held strictly menial jobs in Bladenboro. Spaulding-Monroe School was staffed by a black principal and teachers who received the same dismally low salaries as their white counterparts across town. The principal and his wife lived in a small brick home east of town (the only brick structure there), but most of the teachers lived in a black settlement situated north on the Elizabethtown road. James Robinson operated a dry-cleaning business that was located next to the women's clubhouse directly across the Seaboard Railroad tracks from the Bridger Corporation. A balding, intelligent-looking man, he drew much of his clientele from the mill-owning Bridger family. And north of town lived the Ruffin brothers who were recognized throughout the area as being among the best brick masons. Furthermore, a section crew of the Seaboard Railroad operated east and west out of Bladenboro, maintaining miles of tracks. Supervised by Bennett Buie (a white man) until his death in a rail accident, the six-man crew was entirely black. At one time it included Bill Gillespi's son (Bill, Jr.), a powerful, giant of a man whose muscular development was extraordinary. Although the work of the section crew consisted of heavy, physical labor, a "railroad job" was then considered a "good job." In addition there were black ministers, barbers, hair dressers, and an undertaker who served the black community. Although living together within the parameters of a legally segregated society, the presence of a few black professionals, businessmen and skilled craftsmen undoubtedly affected black-white relations in a positive way. In the case of the Ruffins, for example, whites with brick construction work to be done placed a higher priority on his skill and craftsmanship than on his race.

In such a society where segregation and discrimination were rampant, the potential for violence was always present. This potential was enhanced by the location of Bladenboro in Klan country, that is, in a region where Klan activity was known to occur. Located in Bladen County near the South Carolina line and not too distant from that state's Horry County, the site of much Klan activity in the thirties and forties, Bladenboro was nevertheless free from organizations whose purpose was to control blacks through fear and intimidation. The Klan made no serious effort to penetrate Bladen County around Bladenboro until the mid-fifties. One Saturday night during that decade, I attended a Klan rally underway in an open field immediately east of Bud Edwards' store on NC 211 near the cotton mills. Bud was certainly no racist and I suspect that he allowed the meeting in order to generate business for his store. The speakers were from Horry County and included a fiery-tongued evangelist of hate who was extremely adept at mixing religion with a vicious racism. White-robed and hooded men circulated among the crowd trying, unsuccessfully it appeared, to enlist members to their cause. The most gruesome aspect of the meeting came when a large wooden cross was burned to a very loud, amplified rendition of "The Old Rugged Cross." I sensed from the mood of the crowd that no one was taking the event very seriously. Most of the people present had come out of curiosity and to see a spectacle. If any unit of the Klan was formed in Bladenboro as a result of this or any other meeting, I never heard of it.

In spite of the potential for violence between the races, I recall only one such episode, although there may have been others about which I am ignorant. One Saturday afternoon--the time when area residents came to town to trade, talk, and so on, and when there was the greatest and most frequent contact among blacks and whites--I observed a fistfight between a young teenage black and a teenage white. Urged on by the crowd, the two fought until nearly exhausted. Rather suddenly the young black broke free and began to run, his antagonist and elements of the crowd in hot pursuit. I never shall forget the look of fear on the black's face. Somehow he managed to escape. Although this was potentially a very explosive episode because of the large number of blacks and whites co-mingling on the streets, nothing came of it. In some respect, that nothing developed may be considered an index of the state of race relations in this small rural, cotton-mill town. It seemed that when it came to violence, blacks attacked blacks and whites attacked whites. There was then little violence directed toward each other.

Chapter 3

The Seaboard Airlines Railroad

For youngsters growing up in Bladenboro, one of the most fascinating features of town life was the Seaboard Airlines Railroad, an east-west line connecting Wilmington and Charlotte that divided the town in more ways than one. Unlike today with its vast interstate highway system filled with streaking monstrous trucks hauling the nation's freight, and the massive airport complexes filled with jet aircraft crammed with passengers and freight leaving for and returning from distant, exotic places throughout the world, the thirties and forties relied essentially on the railroads with trains powered by enormous, coal-burning steam (later diesel) engines for freight and passenger services.

The Seaboard was Bladenboro's connection with the outer world, although before World War II there existed harbingers of the escalating changes in transportation that were to mark the postwar era. For example, Grover Pait and Cary Dowless owned small trucking firms, respectively located near their homes on the east and west side of town, whose principal business was hauling packaged yarn for the Bladenboro Cotton Mills to customers located in the Northeast and the South, and hogsheads of tobacco from nearby auction warehouses in Lumberton, Whiteville, and Clarkton to cigarette, cigar, and snuff manufacturers in Piedmont North Carolina. Nevertheless, the mills continued to ship most of its yarn in boxcars and to receive the coal for its huge boilers in hopper cars operating on the Seaboard's rail sidings near the mills.

And the same was true for the Bridger Corporation Store and other stores that largely depended on the railroad for incoming merchandise. A parallel siding north of the Seaboard's mainline ran east through the middle of town onto which was shifted box cars filled with farm implements, fertilizer, stoves, iceboxes (later refrigerators), mules, and dry goods. As the largest general store in Bladenboro, the Bridger Corporation, built in 1911, was the major recipient of such freight. Graham Wilson and Evelyn Thompson in dry-goods, Bernard Ward in appliances, Dewey Guyton in agricultural and hardware goods, and other clerks retailed the goods that arrived by rail. Furthermore, on this rail spur directly east of the outside warehouses of the Bridger Corporation were the stables of H. J. White, a dealer in horses and mules. Each spring White received a rail shipment of mules that he had purchased earlier on buying trips to Missouri. And even before the thirties, the Seaboard had transported the lumber products of sawed lumber, slabs, and turpentine so abundant in the region around town. Historically and economically, this carrier was the lifeblood of the town. However, during the thirties and forties, increasingly trucks from the wholesale houses located in Wilmington and Charlotte (for example, the Thomas Howard Company of Charlotte) made weekly deliveries of many grocery items to the stores, while refrigerated trucks of packing companies, such as Swift & Company, brought weekly supplies of fresh and processed meat. However, despite the inroads of the trucks on rail transportation and the growing ownership of automobiles, the Seaboard remained the principal carrier and connector to the outside world for the people of Bladenboro.

The regular movements of trains over the Seaboard lines helped to established the rhythm of life in Bladenboro. Promptly at ten o'clock each morning, an eastbound passenger/mail train heading for its terminal in Wilmington arrived and paused long enough to discharge and take on passengers, unload and receive bags of mail, and deliver and receive merchandise sent by Railway Express. And at five o'clock in the afternoon, a similar westbound train heading for its Charlotte terminal arrived, causing the ritual of loading and unloading passengers, mail, and merchandise to be repeated again.

Prior to the arrival of the trains, especially in the summertime, the area around the depot platform was marked by a scurrying about of local sightseers, a few passengers, a post-office employee with a small handcart to collect the bags of mail, and a depot worker with a much larger cart to receive incoming merchandise. Further accompanying the daily movements of the trains were all the sights, sounds, and sulfuric odors emitted by coal-burning steam engines (replaced in the post-World War II era by the unique sounds of diesels revving up) that fascinated young and old. However, it was the engines' steam whistle and clanging bell that served as a morning and afternoon time piece for generations of town residents. The warning blasts of the approaching eastbound's whistle west of town near the crossroads at the Bladenboro Cotton Mills announced the time as surely as looking at one's clock. And the same was true in the afternoon when the engineer of the westbound pierced the air with warnings at the road crossings east of town. The east-west runs were a permanent fixture of town life, their dependability comforting to adults and their promise of distant places like Laurinburg, Wilmington, and Charlotte exciting to imaginative youngsters.

Both day and night, the Seaboard helped to structure the life of Bladenboro residents. In between the regular runs of the passenger/mail trains, freight trains composed of loaded and empty boxcars, hopper cars, flat cars, gondola cars stamped with the names of distant rail companies interrupted lazy summer days. One living near the Seaboard line was always aware of the heavy freight traffic it carried. At mid-day and early afternoon, one often saw and heard freight cars being shifted onto the siding either at Bladenboro or the nearby cotton mills. This shifting was a pleasant past-time for idle youngsters and others who enjoyed watching and hearing the intricate positioning and the loud banging of coupling cars. They marveled at the dare-devil antics of brakemen with their striped railroad caps climbing and riding atop freed boxcars while signaling to the engineer whose head and shoulders protruded from the cab. Together engineer and brakemen skillfully shuffled loaded and empty cars into exactly the right position on the siding or back to join the waiting cars left on the mainline. With Front and Back streets sliced by the shifting, pedestrian and vehicular traffic there often came to a standstill until the crew had finished its work and the train, puffing and chugging, had moved on its way. An integral part of the rail panorama was the work of the section crew that operated from a storage shed located adjacent to a siding switch on the westside of Bladenboro. The job of the crew was to maintain a stretch of Seaboard roadbed and track east toward Abbottsburg and Clarkton and west toward Richmond, Butters, and Lumberton. Under the direction of Bennett Buie, who lived directly across the tracks on Back Street, the crew consisted of a half-dozen black laborers. Their work involved back-breaking, physical exertion--muscling crossties into the roadbed, lifting and replacing long, steel rails, anchoring the rails by sledge-hammering spikes into the ties, and using heavy steel pinch bars to inch the rails into position and to firm up the ties in the roadbed. Their work was not for the faint-hearted because it required strength, endurance, and harmony. With a song leader to unify their labor, on cue they moved the heavy steel rails with pinch bars in perfect unison; with hummed orchestration, two crew members with sledgehammers drove rail spikes swiftly into place. Bill Gillepsi, Jr., a powerfully built man with broad shoulders and rippling, muscular biceps, was a typical member of Buie's crew who kept their section of the Seaboard's track safe for traffic. Without men like Gillepsi, the difficult maintenance work would not have been done.

Unlike the train crews who seemed always on the move, black section hands when maintaining the rails near Bladenboro often ate lunch in town. More often than not, of course, they ate on the road near the job site. Weather permitting, in the summer they gathered under the corrugated overhang of the Bridger Corporation store that shaded them from the sun. Laughing, talking, and joking, they ate their lunch, which, if purchased from the store, usually consisted of a substantial, triangular slice of hoop cheese, several large, Nabisco Johnny cakes from a bulk box, and a bottled pint of milk. A few brought their lunches of biscuits, fatback or side meat in emptied lard buckets that they used as lunch boxes. Looking at a Bill Gillepsi devour such food, youngsters wondered how he had become so powerfully built on such a diet. After the meal, the hands would saunter back to the motor-powered rail cart where Buie waited. Climbing on, they were off for a hard afternoon's work before returning in late afternoon.

The daily movement of Buie and his crew was another of those railroad time pieces for the town. Like clockwork, they left at seven in the morning during the summer, their cart pulling a trailer with ties, rails, tools, and whatever was needed for the work of the day. They returned at five, worn out and bedraggled. Because Buie's rail cart had its own distinctive sound that most town residents living near the track easily recognized, its goings and comings became an informal clock by which to measure morning and afternoon hours.

If there was one thing about the Seaboard that seized and held the imagination of all town residents, it was the depot managed by Woody Hilburn, the railroad's agent. During the thirties and forties, the Bladenboro depot was the door that opened to the outside world. Like Azzie's and Charley Bell's barbershops, it also reflected the legally segregated culture then existing in the South. A solid, T-shaped building, it consisted of two segregated, oak-benched waiting rooms (one for "whites" and one for "colored") that formed the top of the T, a warehouse with a platform on its north side for incoming and outgoing merchandise, and a windowed, north-side office for Hilburn that allowed him an unobstructed east/west view of the Seaboard tracks. Located to the west of the depot was a latticed, octagonal gazebo with a bench that gave travelers on the Seaboard an outside choice for waiting. In good weather, ticket holders often gathered under the gazebo while waiting expectantly for the train to arrive. In inclement weather, however, they generally remained in one of the two waiting rooms. For youngsters, the white gazebo became an excellent place for loitering and observing the movement of traffic on the mainline. With shadows partially concealing this vantage point, one noted the daily arrival and departure of passengers, and speculated about the faraway places from which they came and to which they went. And one further observed the prevailing practice of Southern segregation on public carriers. For just as passengers were segregated in the different waiting rooms of the depot, they were also separated while traveling, whites entraining into the "white" car, blacks into the coupled "colored" car. And as the conductor hand-signaled the engineer his cue for departure, from the gazebo one stared out the lattice work at seated black and white passengers, their faces sometimes pressed against the windows of these distinctively racial cars, as the train slowly started on its journey with a jerk. For most white observers, this legal separation was as natural and acceptable as the rising of the sun, but blacks undoubtedly had a different opinion. Perhaps the most interesting part of the depot complex was the office of Woody Hilburn who had a complicated and responsible job. Hilburn, who lived in a large brick house on Back Street within easy walking distance of his work, was a hallmark of punctuality. Like his Front Street friend Levy Bridger, Sr., president of the Bank of Bladenboro, whose short walk each morning to the bank was so precisely timed as to be legendary, one could also judge the hour by the coming and going to work of Hilburn. Once at the depot in his cramped quarters behind the ticket counter, he faced an array of tasks.

On a small table near the windows at the end of the counter, there was a telegraphic device whose key periodically broke out in a furious clicking of messages in Morse code for agents up and down the Seaboard line. Hilburn, a trained telegrapher, ignored much of the traffic in these coded communications because they apparently had nothing to do with his responsibilities at the depot. Consequently, he went about his usual business--selling tickets to passengers, accepting merchandise for shipment from customers, confirming and releasing incoming freight to receivers, supervising the single employee, usually a black man, who assisted around the depot--until his trained ear detected clicks of the key directed to him, a message that he quickly pencil-recorded on paper. More often than not, he immediately acknowledged receipt of the message with a few quick taps on the key, or, if a lengthier response was called for, his sure finger tapped it out rapidly.

Part of Hilburn's job as agent was to communicate with moving freight trains. Some of the messages received in his office were for engineers on trains not scheduled for stops in Bladenboro. Unlike modern trains equipped with devices for communicating while en route, the old steam engines had none, making it necessary for depot agents to pass on to engineers much needed information concerning down-line conditions, the safe operation of the trains, and other matters. Such messages were telegraphed ahead to be delivered by the agent while the train was still in motion. It was not uncommon for Hilburn to perform this feat. Firmly grasping the end of a lightweight hoop shaped like the number nine to which the message was attached, he stood near the track as the train approached at reduced speed and extended the hoop broadside into which the engineer or fireman, leaning out the window of the cab, easily inserted his hand and arm. With the transfer completed from Hilburn to the moving train, the engineer accelerated the train, leaving the station master to go about his regular business at the depot. After watching this maneuver several times, one often wondered what would be the consequences of a miscue in which the transfer was bungled.

There was always a stepped-up pattern of activity around the depot when either a passenger or freight train was arriving, stopping, shifting, departing or passing through Bladenboro. In the late forties shortly before the mail train was scheduled to arrive, a tobacco-chewing George Singletary pushed his cart with outgoing mail bags to the depot where he collected the bags of incoming mail. About thirty minutes following the train's departure when the mail had been "put up," there was an inevitable run of patrons on the nearby post office to "check the mail" in boxes which, in the absence of street delivery service, they had rented; or, to the depot for those persons who expected shipments on Railway Express. With the Front and Back streets blocked by a shifting freight train, delayed traffic built up on both sides of the double tracks of the siding and mainline, causing impatient drivers to seek other crossings on less traveled streets. In the depot's waiting rooms and outside gazebo, ticket holders and the curious waited or milled about expectantly, often checking watches or gazing up-track for signs of the train. And if there was an outgoing shipment of railway express merchandise, Hilburn's helper had it loaded and waiting on the depot's huge cart ready for immediate transfer to the train.

Altogether, the Seaboard railroad injected an element of excitement into the life of Bladenboro that was especially memorable to youngsters who thrived on the sights and sounds it created. They heard the rumble and roar, the hissing steam, the shrill steam whistles and clanging bells of its trains; barefoot, they balanced-walked its rails to avoid sand-spurs thriving between the crossties; they smelled the distinctive odors of burning coal and hot creosote on bridge timbers; they devilishly fired air rifles at the glass insulators holding the telegraph lines that once ran parallel to the tracks; they sat dangerously on trestle abutments as the trains roared by a few feet away, and they jumped crazily off the same trestle into the too shallow waters of Bryant Swamp. But it was in town that the Seaboard made its greatest impact on old and young alike. Without the railroad and the daily stir its traffic created, the town of Bladenboro would have been a dull place indeed.

Chapter 4

Highway NC 211: Road of Entrepreneurs

The major businesses of Bladenboro were, of course located in town. It was here that one found the groceries (Bridger Corporation, Tom Hale's Grocery, Bill and Charles Hussey's Grocery, D. H. Russ's Grocery, and later Dale Hinson's Grocery); the barbers (Azzie Hardin and Charley Bell Ward); the drugstores and doctors' offices (Dewey H. Bridger, Sankey Hutchinson, and Clarencee Bridger); the dry-cleaners (Jodie Bennett and James Robinson); clothiers (Vaught's Cash Store, Dan Freeman, Collins Department Store, and the Bridger Corporation); the Lyric/Wonet theater (W. G. Fussell); the furniture stores (Ed Lewis and Cecil Bennett); the funeral homes (Ed Lewis and Ennis Lewis); the restaurants (Allie Page, Allen Cox, and M. Nance); the car dealers (J. A. Bridger and A. A. White); the service stations (four); the beauty parlor (Elizabeth Dunn); the Bank of Bladenboro (Levi Bridger); the Savings and Loan (Theron Pait); the livery stables (H. J. White); the trucking companies (Grover Pait and Carey Dowless); the attorney (Lloyd Elkins); the bicycle repair shop (Oz Hester); Pelo's Pool Hall; the U. S. Post Office; the Seaboard Railroad Depot; and the offices of the Bladenboro Cotton Mills.

These were the core businesses that fueled the commercial life of Bladenboro and drew hundred of area residents (farmers and mill workers) into town principally on the weekends. They came by car, truck, mule and wagon, and on foot, filling the streets of Bladenboro with people bumping shoulders, laughing, talking, chewing tobacco or dipping snuff, and messing up the streets with colored blotches of sputum. In addition, there were hawkers, principally farmers, on the streets who sold off the beds of wagons or decrepit trucks everything from watermelons and vegetables to boiled and parched peanuts. Even small boys were in business shining shoes and selling newspapers like the Grit. In looking today at the quiet streets of Bladenboro, it is difficult to imagine the throngs of people who spent Saturday in town either on business, such as buying a week's supply of groceries, or just standing around socializing with friends and family members. As a teenager clerking in the Hussey Grocery Store that was located at different times in two locations during the forties, I had a wonderful view of this repeated weekend panorama of a town literally brimful of people. It was a sight to see! Although the schools and churches were segregated during the week, blacks and whites mingled freely and without difficulty on Saturdays in Bladenboro, In the Hussey brothers' grocery, black customers traded side by side with whites, and I am sure that happened in all the other stores, with the possible exception of the barber shops, the pool hall, and eating places that remained white strongholds.

While it is true that the principal commercial life occurred in downtown Bladenboro, highway NC 211, the east-west road that ran through the town and over which hung the town's only stoplight at its intersection with highway NC 410, was the site of many small businesses that reflected the drive of various individuals to better themselves apart from farming or working in the local textile mills. Approximately a half-mile west of town was the Bladenboro Cotton Mills, its company store, and its two villages where hundreds of workers and their families lived. Scores of village residents walked NC 211 into town on Saturday and helped to create the overflow of people described above. Perhaps as a consequence of this weekend movement of humanity along the highway, a number of enterprising individuals created small businesses to exploit the weary pedestrians who walked to and from town, often on the return trip carrying heavy sacks of groceries and sometimes holding a live chicken under an arm.

During this era, if one approached Bladenboro from the west along NC 211, he first encountered the New Mill and its village to the north, and to the south a developing suburb called Pine Ridge that was located across the tracks of the Seaboard Railroad. Sometime during the late forties, Graham Pait, an intelligent, longtime mill employee known for his idiosyncracies and peculiarities, established a small store just across the tracks of the railroad that drew customers primarily from the New Mill village and Pine Ridge. As I recall, the store–something of a convenient store–was very small and short-lived. Off NC 211 and to the north hidden behind the New Mill, Cecil Bennett, the father of two very good friends, had a small store that thrived. Like Pait's store, Bennett's merchandise was principally soft drinks tobacco products, and sundries. However, there were widespread rumors that other unorthodox activities occurred in a back room of the store–perhaps a little gambling and drinking that may have been Bennett's primary source of income. The business lasted only a short while.

After World War II, the Bladenboro Cotton Mills built a store just off NC 211 at the west end of the wooden bridge crossing the mill pond and connecting the Old and New mills. This facility, a small but substantial brick building, was easily accessible to workers who had a few minutes to spare from their machines when, for example, they were being doffed. This store was to replace the "dope wagon," a kind of miniature snack bar or kiosk on wheels that a vendor moved about in the mills through the aisles of whirring spinning frames, cards, and speeders loaded with soft drinks, candy bars, crackers, and headache powders. A corporate enterprise, this store continued until both the Old and New mills were sold and permanently shutdown.

The largest business located on NC 211 was the company store. It, too, was a corporate enterprise that I have discussed in a book entitled "My World Is Gone." Located at the east end of the Old Mill fronting the highway, this full service store was designed to meet practically all the needs of the employees of the Bladenboro Cotton Mills. For example, available in its dry goods section were overalls, shirts, shoes, and bolts of fabrics. On the grocery side of the store were shelves of canned goods, and under the counter, bins of bulk rice, sugar, and beans, and nearby was a showcase for candy, and a soda and ice cream fountain. Located in the back of the building was the meat department where basic cuts of meat were showcased and sold. Also, in the rear was an office where workers could borrow fiat (company) money locally called "Maggie's gold" against their accumulated work time in the mills. For years this store was managed by Emmett Guyton who had formerly clerked in the Bridger Corporation establishment in downtown Bladenboro. As a boy living on the Old Mill village, I visited the company store many times with my father, my Aunt Clara, and often alone when sent by my mother to make a purchase. It did a thriving business and was always crowded near the changing of day shifts in the mills. Many fine people, such as Guyton, Ruby Dunn, and Maggie Bridger, worked in this store, people who remained my friends throughout the rest of their lives. After the sale of the mills, the company store ceased to exist. The new owners physically incorporated the store building into an extension of what had been known as the Old Mill.

Following World War II, Bud Edwards and his wife Magdalene build a small but substantial brick store on the south side of NC 211 on property that Bud had inherited from his parents, the Latt Edwards. Its site near a grove of beautiful long-leaf pines just east of the Seaboard Railroad siding that crossed the highway and ran behind the company store and the Old Mill. Bud was a longtime textile worker who was very well liked and renowned among his fellow workers for his story-telling ability. When he built his store, they became a part of his customer base. Unlike the above privately owned establishments whose merchandise consisted principally of bottled drinks, tobacco products, a smattering of sundries, bread and a few canned goods, the Edwards' store offered the same but differed in that it offered food items from the grill, such as hamburgers, hot dogs, and sandwiches of various kinds. Gasoline was also available. The store was among the first in Bladenboro to sell unleaded gasoline, which my mother bought because she thought it gave extra miles to her old Buick. My most vivid memory concerning Bud and Magdalene's business resulted when visiting Bladenboro in the fifties. On the vacant field next to the store, which was owned by Bud as part of his inheritance, leaders of the Ku Klux Klan from Horry County, South Carolina, held a well-publicized and well-attended recruitment rally that involved about a dozen Klansmen wearing their traditional white paraphernalia and burning a huge cross while loudly playing the hymn, "The Old Rugged Cross." Both sides of NC 211 were lined with cars. I don't think that Bud was a supporter of the KKK, but most likely he permitted the rally on his property because he saw it as a temporary way to enhance his business for the evening. My wife and I attended the rally out of curiosity as, I suspect, did most of the others who were there. It was a memorable sight to behold and an evening to remember. I don't think that the recruiters, who had recently been run out of nearby Robeson County by the Lumbee Indians, had much success in Bladenboro. Years after their deaths, Bud and Magdalene's store is now a small restaurant.

About a quarter-mile east from the Edwards' store, Grad Kinlaw, who was in the lumber business, built a large rectangular, wooden store with an annex during the twenties. When growing up, I don't remember ever having any contact with this business while it was operated by Kinlaw. My father did. It was different with his wife Lucy who owned a milk cow. Lucy sold Grade B milk for ten cents a quart as well as cheap homemade butter. Our family bought her dairy products even though the milk had an onion taste. During the thirties and forties, Grad's building was occupied by several small time entrepreneurs who tried unsuccessfully to make a go of it. There was Cecil Bennett, who was later to open the small store near the New Mill, and Bill Cain, whose business ventures are discussed below, and Clifton Kinlaw.

Cecil was an innovative businessman, using the front part of his store to sell various items such as soft drinks, tobacco products, candy, canned goods, and gasoline. He had a juke box–one of the first that I recall being in Bladenboro–with most country music that resounded throughout the neighborhood at night. He converted the back part of the building into a pool room that consisted of one table, which was not much competition for Pelo's downtown pool hall. There were rumors that when the stored was closed for business, a backroom provided some mill workers who gambled a more convenient place for their poker games than Bryant Swamp where they often gathered on paydays and gambled into the wee hours of the night around a blazing fire. Bill Cain, who already operated a small store on NC 211 across from White Oak Original Free Will Baptist Church, later attempted to expand his business into the Grad Kinlaw building when it was vacated by Bennett. Wartime shortages were probably responsible for the failure of his effort to expand. In 1940, Congress enacted the Selective Service Act which caught up in its net young men like Ferris Hester whose service obligation was then only one year. One evening, Ferris and Vivian Singletary, his new bride, dropped in at Bill's store while Ferris was on leave following basic training. Ferris played a tune entitled "I'll Be Back in a Year Little Darling." He soon returned to camp; the Japanese bombed Pearl Harbor; Ferris was shipped to the Pacific theater of the war; he did not return to Bladenboro for several years. Not long afterwards, Bill went out of business there.

Clifton Kinlaw later operated a store in the building, running the same kind of business as Bennett and Cain. However, he added an ice house, which made it unnecessary to visit the ice plant located near the Old Mill. As I recall, Kinlaw's business extended into the war years and at times was a kind of gathering place for the younger set. I remember one horrible episode of violence there after Hilton Carter, a young mill worker, had engaged in a fist fight with a young marine who was visiting the area on leave. The brawl occurred behind the store, and although the marine gave Carter a terrible whipping, the two apparently reconciled and went inside the store together and purchased Cokes. However, as the marine turned his head, Carter smashed his bottle against the mouth of the marine, knocking out his front teeth. While his victim lay stunned, Carter ran across the Edwards field toward the nearby Old Mill village where he disappeared. When able, the marine followed but was never able to locate Carter. It was probably just as well that he did not. As far as I remember, Clifton Kinlaw was the last proprietor in the building that Grad Kinlaw had built in the twenties.

As noted above, Bill Cain, a tobacco chewing, consumptive looking former mill employee, owned a small store on NC 211 directly across from White Oak Church. Bill was probably the best example of entrepreneurship along the highway. To his small store, he added space for a hamburger stand, which his wife Mollie operated and which did a thriving business especially on the weekends. It was difficult to beat Mollie's burgers and hotdogs at six for a quarter. After spending Saturday in town, very often workers walking back to the mill villages would stop by Bill and Mollie's for a snack before continuing home.

Immediately after the war, Bill attempted to further branch out. Near his store he built a two lane bowling alley. Why he concluded that bowling would be of interest to the customers who ate his wife's hamburgers and hotdogs is a mystery. Perhaps his son Curtis, who had just been released from military service, had something to do with the decision. (Following his return from service, Curtis established a drive-in-theater located just north of town on the Elizabethtown road.) For awhile the new business did well on Saturday afternoon and some evenings. My family and I lived across NC 211 from the bowling alley. It provided me with an opportunity to earn money as a pin setter. Bill charged ten cents per game on each alley. As a pin setter, I received five cents a game, which was very hard work for a nickel. I doubt the two lanes ever covered Bill's costs in establishing this business. It did not last long.

Soon thereafter, Bill decided that what the town needed was a grist mill, the old-time kind of mill involving millstones powered not by water but by electricity. In the late thirties, Will Davis had set up a blacksmith shop and grist mill near the Women's Club building in downtown Bladenboro. However, even then shoeing mules and horses and grinding farmers corn into meal were dying enterprises, but, for some reason, Bill was convinced that he could become an old time, profitable miller. He even learned how to dress the millstones! Once I recall seeing him hard at work with tools dressing the intricate patterns on the bottom and top stones of the mill. By this time, of course, this type of grist milling had long been replaced by large, regional commercial firms that made excellent, refined meal and flour readily available in every grocery store. Obviously, the business was a throwback in time and had no chance of success. Perhaps in setting up the grist mill bill was trying to recapture a part of his youth.

When Ferris Hester, a veteran of World War II in the Pacific theater, returned and resumed his interrupted marriage with Vivian Singletary, the two set up a chicken and egg business slightly off the south side of NC 211 behind the now demolished home of Leland and Rachel Shipman and near the Seaboard Railraod. Throughout the forties the business thrived as the couple sold their products of fryer chickens and eggs to area customers. The business ended with the death of Ferris, but, while it lasted it provided another example of the innovative business motivations of local residents that occurred along NC 211.

Nearer town on the south side of NC 211and near to the present-day Church of God was another very small, interesting business that was a throwback in time. Frank Guyton, an elderly cobbler, operated a shoe repair shop during the depression and war years when shoes were difficult to obtain. I don't know when Guyton set up his little shop where our family sometimes had shoes half-soled or repaired the old-fashioned way, for example, by using a hammer, tacks, and last, or, stitching on an old peddle type sewer. However, like Bill Cain's grist mill, Guyton's craft of cobbling was increasingly obsolete and on its way out. During the war, a more modern shoe repair shop was set up downtown close to Azzie Hardin's barber shop. Its greater efficiency meant a decrease in Guyton's business and ultimately its end. As a teenager, a cousin, Robert Suggs, and I temporarily worked in this new shop on Friday afternoons and Saturdays earning ten cents an hour. With shoes rationed and difficult to obtain during the war, the shop was busy replacing soles, heels, and stitching. Although a few loyal customers continued to use the elderly Guyton's little shop by the side of the road, it was soon out of business and torn down.

Adjacent to and east of Guyton's shop lived Caz Deaver. Deaver was uneducated but, even so, he was an interesting small businessman who ran a small store in a corrugated covered building next to his residence on NC 211. Deaver had his idiosyncracies. My father, who occasionally stopped by the store, which was more like a shed, reported seeing a wooden coffin in the unsealed overhead rafters that Deaver had built for himself and kept in his shop to be used upon his death. Like many store owners, he allowed customers he trusted to buy items on "time." Sadly, his bookkeeping system left much to be desired. Unable to compute with numbers, he resorted to a crude form of pictures in his ledger that represented items that had been purchased by his customers. My father once went to pay a small bill that Deaver had recorded in a circle. Having forgotten what the item was that the circle represented, he assumed that what my father had purchased was a slice of wheel cheese. It was difficult to convince Deaver that the item he had purchased had cost a quarter and that he had not purchased cheese. Upon Deaver's death the business folded.

An empty field separated Deaver's home and shop from A. C. Hardin, who was the father of Luke and Azzie Hardin, the barber. Like most of the other small stores. It sat close to NC 211 and had on overhang that sheltered a single gasoline pump. The pump was the most memorable feature of the store. When one purchased gas from Hardin, it was necessary to hand pump the gas up into an elevated, calibrated glass tank. For example, it one wanted five gallons, one pumped the gas up to the five-gallon hash mark. Gravity would then bring it down into the car's gas tank. Hardin's store contained a similar inventory as the others discussed above–cold drinks, bread, cigarettes and other tobacco products, candy, and a few canned goods. Although this store was situated next to the home of David and Marybelle Pait, an uncle and aunt, I rarely visited the Hardin establishment except to occasionally sit and rest on benches under the overhang when going to or returning from town on hot summer days. This business also ceased when the elderly Hardin died. With so many of these small stores so closely situated on NC 211, it is amazing that each remained in business as long as it did.

Separated from Hardin's store by four private dwellings was the Carey Dowless trucking firm, which was one of two such firms operating out of Bladenboro. The other, also located on NC 211 but on the east side of town, belonged to Grover Pait. Dowless owned several semi trucks and trailers that were in demand by the Bladenboro Cotton Mills, a yarn company that shipped its products by rail and motor transport to fabric mills in Piedmont North Carolina and elsewhere. And when the tobacco warehouses opened in the late summer in Lumberton, Fairmont, Whiteville, and Clarkton where buyers from all the major tobacco companies came for the annual auctions of farmers' tobacco, the several drivers of Dowless–and also those of Pait–were kept busy hauling hogsheads of their purchases to Carolina cities (for example, Winston-Salem) where cigarette, snuff, and chewing tobacco factories were located. For a small town like Bladenboro, the presence of two successful motor transport companies was unusual. At times these companies provided free community services. I remember one episode when H. B. Hargroves, who had volunteered to coach the post-war revival of baseball at Bladenboro High School, persuaded either Dowless or Pait to provide a flat bed truck to take the team to nearby Evergreen where a game had been scheduled but with no school transportation available. Of course, with the passage of time and changes in the Bladenboro Cotton Mills, these small trucking firms went out of business.

Adjacent to the lot where Dowless parked his trucks, a more substantial store than that of Hardin, Deaver, Edwards, or Cain emerged during the war years. It was owned by Albert Thompson who at one time had been sheriff of Bladenboro. I remember this store not only for its unusual design (that is, unusual for the area) but for a personally unfortunate episode involving a rationing stamp for kerosene. Unlike the other small stores along NC 211 that were small and shotgun style in construction, the length of Thompson's store, although rectangular in construction with a high, sloping roof marked by two dormers, was lengthwise and parallel to the highway. Gas tanks of a more modern type than that of Hardin's store were located in front. Like the other stores, the most active business days were Fridays and Saturdays when NC 211 saw scores of pedestrians from the mill villages walking to and from town.

During the war, goods of all kinds were hard to come by and therefore rationed, including products like kerosene and gasoline. It is surprising that any small businesses like Thompson's survived because the large wholesale dealers from Charlotte (for example, Thomas and Howard) tended to supply first their larger customers like the Bridger Corporation and the Hussey Brothers groceries before tending to the needs of the smaller stores. Items, such as sugar, cigarettes, meat, shoes, oil products, etc., were in short supply and occasionally caused tension between store owners and their customers. Once I purchased a gallon of kerosene at Thompson's store, which required a rationing stamp that I dutifully surrendered. The price of the kerosene was placed on my father's charge account. When he later attempted to pay his bill, Thompson asked for a rationing stamp, indicating that he had not received one at the time of purchase. Knowing that I had already give the stamp, my father refused to provide another, a refusal that led to harsh words and nearly a brawl between the two men. This was not an isolated episode, for I later discovered while working in the Hussey Brothers grocery that wartime shortages involving rationing stamps often led to unusual tensions between shop owners and their customers. Later, during the fifties Thompson moved his business across the highway to the intersection of Butler Mill Road and NC 211. Sometime after his death, the store ceased to exist.

Perhaps the most notorious business that developed on NC 211 was the Eagle Eye that was located about a tenth of a mile east of Albert Thompson's original store. It was the nearest thing to a "honky tonk" establishment existing in Bladenboro during my youth. It was a place that parents warned their boys to avoid, for it was considered to be much worse than Pelo's pool hall. There were rumors that a lot of evil things went on there–like drinking beer and whiskey. On Friday and Saturday afternoons, it was not unusual for pedestrians en route to and from town to hear loud music from a juke box and loud, boisterous laughing and talking emanating from the Eagle Eye, indicating that its patrons, perhaps having had a little too much to drink, were having a wonderfully "good time." And it was not uncommon for patrons, some of whom had obviously too much whiskey or beer, to mill around outside the business. It was a place where fights and other disturbances sometimes occurred, making it necessary for the police to be called. As a teenager, I sometimes walked with my father past the Eagle Eye. He was highly critical of the events that went on there. Consequently, he deliberately crossed over to the opposite side of NC 211 when he saw unruly customers milling about outside. He didn't want any chance encounter that might lead to his involvement with any drunk. I don't think that the Eagle Eye was locally owned. As I recall, two out-of-town men were proprietors of the business until it folded. Later on, Allie Page; who at different times operated restaurants in Bladenboro, opened a small sandwich shop in a portion of the building, which no longer exists.

Toward the closing of World War II, Smithy Edwards built a small eating establishment off NC 211 east of the Eagle Eye and near the bridge built by the Public Works Administration (PWA) that crossed Bryant Swamp into Bladenboro proper. Smithy was a veteran of the navy who had been released from duty on torpedo boats because he had developed a heart condition. Smithy's restaurant, more like today's snack bars, was an interesting place. In the immediate postwar years when meat became more plentiful, especially beef, it had the reputation of serving the best hamburgers in town. Unlike Mollie Cain's hamburgers, which consisted of hamburger meat mixed with a liberal amount of "light bread" and a slice of tomato so thin that it was translucent (making it possible for her to sell them at six for a quarter), a Smithy burger consisted of a generous, thick ground-round beef patty, loaded with lettuce and tomato and sold for ten cents each. When my family wanted a burger, I would be sent to Smithy's for three of his delicious burgers.

I always enjoyed going into Smithy's place of business. There were often interesting people there to whom I tried to sell–often unsuccessfully–the Grit newspapers. Once I fell into a conversation with an elderly man named Hill who seemed to be caught up in a wave of self-pity and nostalgia. He made a remark that I have never forgotten. What provoked his comment has escaped my memory. "Son." he said, "the tragedy of life is old age." I had to wait fifty or more years to fully understand what he meant by that remark. Smithy himself was an interesting person. He was a drummer who kept a set of drums at the business. On days when trade was slow, Smithy practiced on his drums and unleashed his pent up energies as only a rabid lover of drumsticks can do. If on the inside, it was fascinating to watch him; if on the outside, the noise erupting from his shop demanded one's attention. The sites formerly occupied by the Eagle Eye and Smith's shop are now the location of other businesses.

Graham Pait, Cecil Bennett, Bud Edwards, Grad Kinlaw Billl Cain, Clifton Kinlaw, Ferris Hester, Frank Guyton, Caz Deaver, A. C. Hardin, Carey Dowless Albert Thomson, Smithy Edwards, and others–all were entrepreneurs who started small business enterprises in the worst of times (depression and wartime scarcity) along NC 211, running west from the bridge crossing Bryant Swamp to the end of the New Mill, a distance of less than a mile and a half. Unlike today when financial assistance might have been available from the Small Business Administration and other sources to aid startup enterprises such as these, these individuals relied entirely upon their own resources for whatever capital was needed. None of them had surplus finances to draw upon. Furthermore, few of them had even the rudiments of a high school education. And they certainly were not aware of market trends as Bill Cain's failed enterprise of grist milling indicated. Nevertheless, these obstacles did not deter them from reaching out and engaging in economic activities beyond the cotton mills where some of them or their wives had worked and where most people living west of Bladenboro seemed bound for the rest of their lives. In many ways the individuals noted above were an admirable bunch in that they strived to make their lives better by assuming risks when it was not easy to do so. They were truly entrepreneurs of NC 211!

Chapter 5

Bladenboro's White Public Schools

When I began attending the Bladenboro Public Schools in 1935 as a first-grade student, it was already one of the largest consolidated school systems in North Carolina. Prior to my arrival as a student, a number of small county schools had merged into substantial elementary and high schools located on the same campus at the south end of town at the juncture of NC 131 and NC 410. As late as the early forties during World War II growth in enrollment continued when the Abbottsburg school burned and its students were incorporated into the Bladenboro system. As a consequence of these consolidations, out-of-town children from nearby farms and the two mill villages were bused in each morning. For children living within two miles of the schools state law then required them to walk or have their parents provide their transportation. At the beginning of my school career I was unaffected by this rule.

I recall a small fleet of yellow buses, owned and maintained by Bladen County, parked daily in a large empty lot outside the elementary building. Although unusual by today's standards of safety, these buses were driven by responsible high-school students fortunate enough to have drivers' licenses. (Incidentally, they and their counterparts in other state schools compiled one of the best safety records in the nation among school bus drivers whether adults or students.) They were paid a pittance for their service. Upon completion of the final route of the day, the buses were parked overnight at the homes of the drivers in readiness for the next day's run. During the summer, most buses were parked in a county motor pool near Elizabethtown where they were, if needed, repaired and readied for the next school year. Cooper Ransom, an uncle, worked as a mechanic maintaining these buses. For much of my first school year, I escaped the busing experience because of where my family lived in a rented house in Bladenboro.

Hard times during the Great Depression made life difficult for most families and ours was no exception. In 1933 our family left a rented house on the Old Mill village (where I had spent several months in a pre-school sponsored by the mill and the federal government) and moved for the winter out to my Grandfather Asie Suggs's farm on the Dublin road. In the following Spring we moved again, this time into temporary rooms in the Hale's house owned by Artie Suggs, an uncle. This house was located in Bladenboro facing the Seaboard Railroad and adjacent to "Hen" Freeman, an accountant for the Bladenboro Cotton Mills, and Leck Hales, assistant postmaster. From this site, the distance to the elementary school was less than a half-mile. When school began in the Fall of 1935, I joined the Freemen and other town children, principally members of the Bridger families who lived on Front Street, and walked to school. A similar movement of children occurred on Back Street. And, of course, the buses brought loads of students from the surrounding farms and the mill villages.

The elementary school, which today houses the Bladenboro Historical Museum, was a rectangular, two-story brick building that contained sixteen classrooms (eight on each floor), an administrative office, and an auditorium large enough to seat all the students. The structure was heated in the winter by steam running through radiators generated by a coal-fired furnace. Until well heated, these radiators made loud, clanking noises as if someone was banging on the pipes with a hammer. While I was in grade school, the man who was responsible for firing the furnace to keep the building warm, and who also had janitorial duties in the boys and girls toilets was an African-American named Oscar. If he had other maintenance responsibilities, I failed to note them. The building did require substantial upkeep. Upon their return each Fall, the students found that crews had oiled the pine floors and that for awhile the darken floors exuded an oily odor. There were other signs that work had been done to the building over the summer. Because there were no drinking fountains inside the building, students drank from a row of spigots located outside at the south end of the building. On the outside there was an expansive playground which, during recess, was filled with playing children, in most instances, games of their own choosing, for example, marbles, tag football, games of chase, and occasionally a few fights. For the smaller children, there were several slides and swings, too few for the numbers involved. (Today much of the former playground today is covered in a paved parking lot to serve the new middle school and the Historical Museum.)

Bladenboro High School was located on the south side of the campus. It faced the elementary school that was located approximately one hundred yards to the north. The high school was a brick, T-shaped building containing eight classrooms, an administrative office, and an auditorium with space behind its stage for a small library. (In recent years, the high school has been incorporated into a new middle school.) This building, especially during the war years, was the focus of community life, sale of war bonds, and so on. Behind the high school was a wooden structure where agricultural subjects were taught to students interested in becoming future farmers. A number of my classmates intended to make farming a career choice. And in 1943, the year that I entered high school, there was a large wooden gymnasium that had been built during the thirties as a PWA/WPA project, one of several such projects undertaken in Bladenboro. It was used not only for boys and girls basketball but also to store a few buses during the summer months when school was not in session, a procedure that did not help the floor. A wooden ramp connected the gymnasium to the wooden stands of an adjacent ball park, the field of which was surrounded by a wooden fence. The echoing crack of bats on balls made a wonderful sound in that enclosure. Unfortunately, during the summer of 1943, the accumulated trash under the stands was mysteriously ignited and the fire spread to the adjacent gymnasium and fence. The fire destroyed everything but a section of the fence. Rumors spread that the town's volunteer fire department might have saved the facility had not a leading citizen demanded that the fire hose running from a hydrant across NC 131 be disconnected in order that his car might pass. For those of us entering high school that Fall who looked forward to playing basketball, the loss of the gymnasium was a devastating blow. Fortunately, the fire was contained before it spread to the nearby high school and the agricultural building.

Shortly after World War II and prior to the graduation of the Class of 1947, school authorities ordered constructed a new educational building on the east side of the campus that contained classrooms and a cafeteria. Before the cafeteria, students brought their lunches from home or did without. A few students who lived in the immediate vicinity of the school (for example, Harold White a classmate who lived across Front street from the school) were permitted to go home for lunch. Before the opening of the new cafeteria, there was a short period when milk, pastries, and crackers were available from a basement room located in the elementary building, a very unsatisfactory, makeshift arrangement. As I recall, Mrs. Foster Smith was placed in charge of the cafeteria where students might eat low-cost, nutritious meals that were made possible by utilizing available government assistance in the form of food surpluses. And the cafeteria was used for other functions than school lunches. For example, the Class of 1947–my class–held its senior banquet in the new facility.

In later years major structural changes occurred on the campus of the Bladenboro Public Schools. The old high school building was incorporated into an enlarged renovated facility, with the old building remaining clearly evident. The large elementary building remained the same. It was in this older building that dozens of classmates and I began our public education in 1935 in the midst of the Great Depression.

With the exception of a few students, class pictures taken during that era reveal a bedraggled looking bunch of youngsters whose faces and clothing reflected the "hard times" that their families were enduring. Fortunately, there was then a corp of hard-nosed professional teachers–entirely women with one exception, a Mr. Poplin–who then taught the classes of farm, mill, and town children. Their word was law in the classroom and, consequently, there were few discipline problems because the instructors were in charge, not the students. Furthermore, a whipping or punishment in school usually meant a whipping or additional punishment upon returning home by parents who generally valued education and rarely questioned the actions of teachers or principals who disciplined their children. The result of that discipline was that time in the classroom was focused on learning.

My classmates and I had exceptional elementary teachers whose names I remember and cherish–Knox, Brown, Stone, McLauren, Tatum, Pierce, Hall, Meggs, and others. They taught the basics of reading, spelling, arithmetic, geography, history, writing, and music in a demanding but interesting manner. Under these teachers, a student found it difficult not to learn unless he was an intellectual dud. Within the same elementary building, year after year a progression of students went from the first to the eighth grade having one excellent teacher after another. For those of us entering the Bladenboro Public Schools in 1935, the quality of our teachers and their work did not become self-evident to many of us until after the outbreak of World War II when many teachers, especially at the secondary level, were drafted into the military services.

Unlike today when technological innovations such as computers flood the classrooms so rapidly that teachers find it difficult to stay competent in these developments, and unlike today when teachers have become surrogates for parents, churches, and society in teaching values and behavior, and unlike today when teachers confront students with medical, mental, racial, and language problems with the expectations that all students can learn equally well, and unlike today when children increasingly come from broken homes, remarriages, and mixed, joined families, and unlike today when students are beset by a thousand distractions, Bladenboro elementary teachers of the thirties and forties confronted classes of heterogeneous students from the farms, mill villages, and town (many of us fortunate to be in school) who, whether they liked it or not, behaved themselves, listened, and learned from instructors who tolerated no nonsense. Such a disciplined background tremendously benefitted learners prior to entering high school in 1943 in the midst of World War II.

Sometime during 1941, the North Carolina legislature expanded the number of years for graduation from high school from eleven to twelve years. Unfortunately, instead of adding a new twelfth grade, authorities inserted a new eighth grade, a decision that delayed my classmates and I from entering high school until 1943 and eliminated a class from graduating in 1946. As a result, in addition to contending with the natural staffing problems caused by the war, the administration of Principal A. A. White had to contend with the incorporation of this new eighth grade into the curriculum. The Class of 1947 was thus the first to participate in this new arrangement. As I recall, the addition of the new eighth grade added nothing substantive to the school's curriculum. A Miss Hall, its teacher, simply moved with our former seventh grade class from the elementary to the high school building where her students essentially repeated anew a study of seventh grade subjects.

However, the curriculum of the high school offered a range of subjects that allowed a student to focus on agricultural courses, college prep courses, or general education. Every student was required to take four courses in English, an American history course, an optional course in science (biology, physics, or chemistry), an optional course in math (general arithmetic, Algebra I & II, geometry), a language course (Latin or Spanish), and an elective courses (music, sociology, economics, or agriculture). If properly taught the curriculum offered students an opportunity to obtain a strong secondary school education. Unfortunately, however, World War II was to wreak havoc upon the potential reflected in the courses composing the curriculum. Several illustrations indicate the instructional problems caused by the war.

A. A. White, who ran the white Bladenboro Public Schools and who served as principal of the high school until after the war, had a difficult time finding competent teachers for the more difficult subjects in science and math, and he was plagued with turnovers on his staff. Locals were frequently brought in as substitutes or as long-term instructors, individuals like Mrs. Mary Ida Bridger, Mrs. Mary Elise Bridger, Mrs. Susie Hutchinson, Mr Ippie Pait, and others. Departures of teachers often led to interesting instructional situations. For example, when Nettles who taught physics and math unexpectedly resigned, his geometry class, a one-semester course, endured three different teachers, neither of whom was competent in the subject matter. Consequently, when each new instructor was thrown into the breach, especially the last two, students began anew with the first chapter of the text, which was the extent of the coverage for the semester. Another example was physics. The original teacher, the same Mr. Nettles, was an able teacher, however, he was confronting personal problems and seemed to be an unhappy man. When he resigned, the school's commercial teacher, a Miss Eury, was assigned the task of continuing the course. After confessing to the class that she knew nothing about physics, certainly did not know how to teach the subject matter, for an hour each day she sat and read from "Girl of the Limberlost." With the end of the war in 1945, the school year began with the hiring of a new teacher with the responsibility of teaching chemistry and coaching a renewed sports program. Except for baseball that H. B. Hargroves, a volunteer coach, had managed, there had been no sports at Bladenboro High School during the war years of 1943-1945. Coaching boys and girls basketball without a gymnasium, restarting a football program, and taking over an on-going baseball program from Hargroves was a tough assignment even without the responsibility of teaching chemistry. Considering the difficulties he faced, the new coach and out-of-town teacher did reasonably well as a coach, but despite having a degree in biochemistry from a private college, he was definitely not a chemistry teacher. Furthermore, the "lab" he inherited was full of dangerous chemicals, improperly labeled with none of the necessary safeguards to protect students had the substances actually been used. Fortunately, there were no serious accidents during his one year tenure.

Although World War II made it difficult to maintain a high-school teaching staff equal in quality to that of the pre-war elementary school, there were several excellent secondary teachers. Miss Dorothea Farmer, home-room teacher and counselor for the Class of 1947 for three years, was also an excellent English teacher who took great interest in the success of all her students. For a few students who were interested in languages, she also taught Latin or Spanish as an elective on an individual basis. Of the three science courses offered in the school, the only one that had much substance was biology. It was taught by Miss Marjorie MacKenzie, a recent college graduate who had somehow found her way to Bladenboro High School. Young and pretty, she was a favorite of the boys, a fact that did not reduce her seriousness about biology or her efforts to teach it effectively. In spite of inadequate lab facilities and teaching materials, she made the subject interesting. Miss Eury, the commercial teacher who taught typing and business arithmetic, was also an effective teacher in those subjects. And Mrs. Mary Ida Bridger, a local resident whom White had recruited to teach Algebra I and II was recognized as a very good algebra instructor. There were undoubtedly others who impressed individual students as being able and competent teachers.

With the ending of the war in 1945, with the retirement of White, and the return of veteran teachers into the classrooms, the instructional corps at the high school changed. W. A. Hough replaced White as principal/administrator, Robert Randall became the new coach while teaching sociology and economics, Edgar Bridger replaced in math Mrs.

Mary Ida Bridger, a Mrs. Knight replaced Mr. Ippie Pait as an English teacher, and a Mr. Perkins replaced Mrs. Alese Bridger who had taught music and other courses. As a result of these and other immediate postwar changes, the instructional staff was very different throughout the closing years of the forties.

When one considers the difficulties imposed on public education during the tumultuous war years when administrators competed with defense industries for the available civilian talent to serve as teachers (whose salaries were often less than individuals working in war production), it is remarkable that the Bladenboro Public Schools performed as well as they did. Some of the individuals, especially local people, who stepped in to fill the classroom during that era of instructor shortage may not have been very skilled at teaching. However, they were dedicated to keeping the schools operating during a time of national crisis, and they undoubtedly did the best they could under trying circumstances. Without their willingness to serve, the lives of many students would certainly have been changed and certainly not always for the better.

There was more to Bladenboro High School than formal education. As in most public schools during the wartime and immediate postwar forties, extra-curricular activities were severely curtailed because not long after the start of the international conflict, growing shortages occurred in nearly everything that supported a rural school like that of Bladenboro. For example, gasoline was in short supply for its fleet of buses that brought the majority of students in from the countryside, a function far more important than transporting the baseball, football, or basketball teams to play elsewhere. As a result of the war and the burning of the gymnasium and ball park stands, these sports were curtailed and not renewed until 1945 when, with the hiring of a new general coach, old football equipment that had been stored under the high school auditorium was retrieved and portions used for the first several games that Fall. During the seasons of 1945-1947, basketball practice occurred on a dirt surface, except for an occasional train ride to nearby Clarkton where that school's officials graciously allowed the Bladenboro team limited practice time. Needless to say, under the circumstances there were not many victories for a team with no gymnasium. The situation in football and baseball was somewhat different. There was evidence that the school was athletically emerging from the wartime doldrums when the school purchased new football and baseball uniforms. By the Spring of 1947, under Robert Randall, the new coach, the school was fielding properly clad football teams, and baseball teams, and both boys and a girls basketball teams. It was several years before the school acquired a new gymnasium.

There was also a resurgence in other extracurricular activities, particularly after the war's end. While substituting Mrs. Alese Bridger, who loved music and played the piano with a flourish, taught group singing as an elective, focusing long periods, as I recall, on two compositions–"McNamara Band" and "The Road to Mandalay." In the Fall of 1945, a Mr. Perkins replaced Mrs. Bridger in teaching choral music to interested students. And that same Fall, a Mr. Womble, a fragile, skinny man with impaired vision who had previously attempted to improve the physical condition of the entire student body by teaching calisthenics, now attempted to organize a marching band that consisted of about six or eight students with absolutely no musical experience or talent. I was in the band. The attempt was a failure though the students did the best they could with poor leadership and no talent. There were other extracurricular opportunities. The school had a Beta Club to which any student with a "B" average at the end of his junior year might join. Under the sponsorship of Miss Dorothea Farmer, the club was active in school affairs and, at least on one occasion, the club traveled to Winston-Salem to a state convention where the club members presented a humorous skit. Under the direction of a John Elam, there was also a Future Farmers Club that attracted students interested in agricultural careers. The club was active and sent representatives to various local and state meetings. In addition to these students organizations, teachers sponsored class plays that involved students who were juniors and seniors.

Although World War II cast a shadow over high-school life by limiting principally sports activities, it also opened up other avenues for student expression. Because of the food shortages, the government encouraged all citizens to have "victory gardens" to increase the nation's food supply. Directed by Mrs. Alese Bridger, her class in health produced a large "victory" garden using a plot located behind the agricultural building. There were other shortages during the war. Metals of all kinds were in demand for the war effort. Everyone was encouraged to surrender any scrap metal they might have. On a few occasions upperclassmen were released from the high school to participate in scrap metal drives, usually accompanying a truck driver out to someone's farm for a load of scrap. And in the early stages of the war when blackouts were being imposed even on small towns such as Bladenboro out of fear of possible air raids, a spotting station for aircraft was placed on top of the elementary building, manned by upperclassmen, to report the flight and direction of any plane seen over the area. And, of course, the school sponsored the sale of war bonds and war stamps (convertible to bonds), although the students were minor participants in these events. These activities enriched the lives of the students during the crisis of war by allowing them to participate and feel that they were part of the war effort.

The decades of the thirties and forties, a time of national depression and international war, were not the best of times anywhere for public education. All things considered, it is amazing that a large consolidated rural school like that in Bladenboro did as well as it did in educating local children. Unlike today when all kinds of technological aides are available for classroom teachers, who nevertheless daily face insurmountable problems, none of these devices were then available for teachers. For example, throughout most of the forties, the Bladenboro schools had only one film projector that was sometimes used on Friday afternoons to show what someone judged to be an educational film, that is, if the student could somehow come up with a dime, the admittance fee. On the day that Franklin D. Roosevelt made his famous "day of infamy" speech requesting the Congress to declare war against Japan, assembled students in the high-school auditorium heard the speech over a Philco console radio brought into the school and set on the stage. And there were times when students in both the elementary and high school were allowed to leave school in the middle of the day and amble down Front Street to W. G. Fussell's Lyric Theater to view special showings of movies like "Gone with the Wind" and "Chopin," that is, if the students came up with the money for the movie. Such excursions were attempts to make available some enrichment in the lives of students, many of whom lacked access to radios or daily newspapers. When placed in the context of the times, the education that a student received in the Bladenboro Public Schools was as much as one could reasonably expect.

At this time Southern society was extremely segregated and this was true in public education. "Whites" had their schools; "Blacks" had theirs. Consequently, the above overview of the Bladenboro Public Schools is that of the white schools, which I attended. Spaulding-Monroe School for black children was located about one-half mile east of town off NC 211. Like the white schools, most of its students were bused in from the surrounding countryside. Paradoxically, buses filled with white children would daily pass Spaulding-Monroe en route to their school, while buses filled with black children would pass the white school en route to their school. The school separation of the races was taken for granted by both races because most major institutions were then segregated–for example, even the passenger trains of the Seaboard Railroad and even the churches of the same denomination. While there was much co-mingling on the streets and in stores among whites and blacks–and even strong friendships–there was the instinctive awareness that there were both legal and informal limits restricting the relationships between the races. As a result, despite the fact that white and black schools were in the business of educating children of the community, there was little or no contact between the professional staffs of the schools and certainly no student contact in sports or social activities. It is for this reason that there is no commentary about the substance or quality of the education received by black children. Other than members of the Bladen County Board of Education few whites knew little if anything about activities within Spaulding-Monroe and few blacks knew little if anything about activities with the white school. This situation of mutual ignorance would not change until much later.

Chapter 6

Azzie's and Charlie Bell's Barbershops

Every small town has a barbershop, and Bladenboro was no exception. Actually, within the town limits there were two barbershops to serve white patrons, but there was none for blacks. In Bladenboro as throughout the South, during the thirties through the fifties the races did not co-mingle as customers in barbershops, restaurants, or other businesses providing personal services. Once and awhile, a white barber might hire a black as a shoeshine boy, that is, if a willing, poor white teenager, usually from the cotton mill village, was unavailable to fill the spot. The prevailing white perception was that black males, whether a teenager or an adult, made excellent shoeshine boys because of their natural rhythm and their ability to set the shine cloth swishing and popping as they converted shoe leather into mirrors. The music from the cloth fascinated and entertained customers who waited for chairs to open or for a favorite barber to become free. For this reason, black males were occasionally found working as shoeshine boys in the town's barbershops, a job that also entailed sweeping up the mounds of snipped hair and cigarette butts that gradually littered the floor as the day progressed, and tending to the toilet and shower facilities in the back of each shop. Not even World War II, which had led to much racial mixing in defense industries like the Wilmington shipyards, disturbed this traditional separation of the races in the barbershops of Bladenboro.

The most patronized of the white shops belonged to Azzie Hardin who had begun barbering shortly after his discharge from the army following World War I. Sandwiched between Roger Russ's Grocery and Pelo's Pool Hall in a block-long building owned by James Albert Bridger, proprietor of the Bridger Motor Company and a power in Bladen County's Democratic politics, Azzie's shop fronted NC 211 that ran east-west through the town. Through the shop's large plate glass window, a customer sitting in Azzie's front chair could see and feel the loaded trucks and oil tankers that rumbled along this narrow roadway that cut through the heart of town. And if in Azzie's chair on Friday or Saturday, he was positioned to watch the hordes of people scurrying past the window.

Charley Bell Ward owned the other white barbershop. Charley Bell had begun his career as a barber during the twenties. His shop was in a corner-block building owned by Dr. Dewey H. Bridger, one of two physicians in town. The shop looked out on Front Street, the other principal thoroughfare running north-south through the heart of town, and was squeezed between Tom Hales's Grocery and the Bridger Drug Store. A wooden stairway led up to the second-floor offices of the Bladenboro Cotton Mills and separated the shop from the drugstore.

For more than forty years, working in friendly competition less than a block from each other on perpendicular streets that crossed under the only stoplight in town, Azzie and Charley Bell snipped the hair and shaved the faces of several generations who were born, raised, and lived in this small community. During the week when business was slow, each barbered alone, with the extra chairs standing unused. But on the weekends, each called in extra help to serve the hordes of people who flooded the town.

On Friday afternoon and all day Saturday, people from the mill villages situated about a mile to the west off NC 211 and farmers from the surrounding countryside streamed into town by the scores, traveling by car, mule and wagon, and on foot. Groceries for the next week had to be bought; friends had to be seen; family news had to be shared; and hair had to be trimmed for church, for social events, and for the coming weeks. On weekends, the streets of Bladenboro teemed with people who had no other place to go to break the monotony of everyday life. They clustered leisurely in groups, squatting on the streets, leaning on buildings or power poles, sitting under the awnings of the Bridger Corporation store facing the Seaboard Railroad--chewing tobacco, dipping snuff, spitting, whittling, talking, talking, talking, always talking about the weather, farming, conditions in the cotton mills, religion, family, baseball, the depression, the war--the groups constantly in transition, losing and replacing members as the day wore on. For most mill hands and farmers the trip into Bladenboro was an essential weekend ritual that was vital to their psychic well-being. "Goin' to the 'Boro'" removed them from the noise and discipline of the mill or the isolation of the farm and, for awhile, pushed aside their worries over either the depression or the war.

Although Azzie and Charley Bell engaged in friendly competition for uncommitted customers, each had his own clientele of regulars. Azzie's clientele consisted principally of mill hands drawn from the two villages of the Bladenboro Cotton Mills west of town and a scattering of small farmers, many of whom also worked in the mills during winter months when work was available. There were reasons why mill hands patronized Azzie's shop. Although Azzie's father A. C. Hardin was the proprietor of a very small store and filling station located west of town on NC 211 half-way between town and the Bladenboro Cotton Mills, all of his sons--Azzie, Oak, and Luke--and their families had worked in the nearby mills. However, upon marrying the sister of a downtown merchant named Dan Freeman, Azzie quit the mills and became a barber. Azzie's brother Luke had two sons, Bernice and Houston, who, like most of the children of mill hands in the thirties and forties, took jobs as mill hands as did their wives, that is, when work was available. They accepted work in the cotton mills as their lot. Furthermore, in the twenties and early thirties when they were young, Azzie, Oak and Luke were regular, outstanding players on the mill's baseball team called the Spinners that was part of a textile league in the eastern Carolinas. And, although the Hardin brothers moved off the village, Azzie into a home on Back Street, and Luke to a home on NC 211, their work and previous play on the mill baseball team made them well-known among fellow workers and the residents of the villages. Their leaving the mills and moving elsewhere, therefore, did not adversely affect their "you're-one-of-us" status with village residents. They were accepted and remained acknowledged members of the working-class community. For Azzie, his mill connections paid off in customers who patronized his shop rather than Charley Bell's. Azzie was in tune with the feelings and aspirations of workers; he spoke their language and was part of their culture; he identified with their problems; and he loved baseball.

During the baseball seasons, his shop radio stayed tuned into games of the St. Louis (Browns) Cardinals or the Boston Red Sox--never the New York Yankees, except, of course, when the Yankees played Boston, or, when the Yankees played in the World Series! With few radios in their homes, baseball-loving mill hands often filed into the crowded shop on Saturday afternoons to listen and to enjoy the game during their long wait for a haircut or shave. In the forties, baseball took their minds off problems in the mills and the war. They were Azzie's largest clientele. As textile workers or "lint-heads," they were also among the least influential people in the area, in the minds of some town residents just above the blacks or perhaps in the same class. However, at Azzie's shop, they felt at home.

Charley Bell drew the bulk of his customers from area farmers, store clerks, and members of the large Bridger family who lived in the attractive, beautiful houses on Front Street, and who owned the Bladenboro Cotton Mills and nearly everything else in town--the land, the buildings, the bank, the car dealership, and much of the farmland in the surrounding area. Unlike Azzie, Charley Bell was not part of the mill culture. However, he was very much a part of the life of the small farmers who patronized his shop. He was one of them. He owned a small farm located several miles to the east off NC 211 between Bladenboro and Abbottsburg where he and his family cultivated a small acreage of tobacco and corn. Farmers were drawn to his shop just as mill hands were drawn to Azzie's. Charley Bell was both a barber and a farmer, although barbering consumed most of his waking hours. Everyday, like clockwork, he drove into town and opened his shop for business, and like Azzie, patiently sat in the front chair while waiting for the sporadic customers that wandered in during the weekdays.

It was during the week that Charley Bell serviced the most influential and well-to-do people in town, individuals like Joe Bridger, president of the Bladenboro Cotton Mills, or Levy Bridger, Sr., president of the Bank of Bladenboro, or James A. Bridger, president of the Bridger Motor Company, or Dr. Dewey H. Bridger, one of two physicians in town, or "Liv" Bridger, president of the Bridger Corporation Store. "Old Man Joe," as the mill hands called him, regularly dropped in from his upstairs office above the shop, and after positioning himself comfortably in the front chair, sat and munched tobacco while Charley Bell meticulously worked away with scissors and hand clippers on his nearly bald head.

Bridger, a large man, occasionally arose and stepped ponderously to the nearby front door, opened it, and spat out a stream of tobacco juice onto the sidewalk, forcing Charley Bell to pause in his work until, Mr. Joe, his most important customer had again settled comfortably into the chair. The haircut was usually followed by a ritual shave, during which Old Man Joe, now momentarily free of tobacco juice and stretched full-length in the chair, dozed off into a catnap under the relaxing influence of hot towels and the pampering of his barber. The Bridger clan was large and it provided a steady and reliable source of income because the members of the family cared about their appearance, especially those who managed the various enterprises in town. Furthermore, Charley Bell's shop provided a measure of insulation from the mill hands, most of whom patronized Azzie's shop. When Friday and Saturday rolled around, the bench in Charley Bell's shop was likely to be full, just as was that in Azzie's shop. Farmers came from all around and most of those wanting haircuts went to Charley Bell's shop where they found people like themselves with whom they talked quietly about common problems on the farm. There was no noisy radio broadcasting a baseball game, nor boisterous talk about the standing of the local team in the textile league, nor conversation about wages in the mill, and so on. There was much talk about the weather, crops, prices on corn and tobacco, the war, and so on. And sometimes, there would be little conversation at all, the customers being content, if the week had been particularly difficult, just to sit quietly or perhaps doze while waiting their turn in the chair. On the weekends, the aura in Charley Bell's shop was marked by a quiet dignity not found in Azzie's shop. Charley Bell, who was a soft spoken rather quiet man, contributed to this atmosphere. Unlike many barbers, he felt no compulsion to entertain his customers. Instead, he tended to remain focused on his work. Occasionally, however, if he had had a good day fishing with a friend like C. A. Shaw, who managed Bridger's Drug Store next door, he loved to tell about his catch.

Azzie's shop was very different on the weekends as workers from the mills crowded in for haircuts, to catch up on the news, to listen to ball games, and to noisily socialize while they sat on a long oak bench waiting their turn. For many of them, the visit to town was an important weekly escape from the mill and the village. Because few of them had radios, Azzie's shop was a news and sports center, a place where they caught up on what was happening in the world. The shop was therefore far noisier than Charley Bell's, full of jokes, laughing, outrageous gossip and rumors of scandals, misery tales of depression and war, and renewal of conversations among fellow workers involving subjects that had been talked about for days during shift changes at the mill. Unlike Charley Bell's, Azzie's shop was filled with boisterous noise from the radio, customers and the shoeshine boy.

Furthermore, because none of the mill workers had indoor plumbing in their rented houses on the villages, some of them came to use the showers located in the back of the shop that provided an opportunity for a weekly, refreshing scrubbing. It was not uncommon--much more common than at Charley Bell's shop, which also had shower facilities in the back--for a customer to enter Azzie's shop with fresh clothing to be worn after showering at the shop. This was often followed by the full treatment--haircut, shave, tonic, facial, and shoeshine. The end result was the transformation of the customer, one who came in looking like a bum but left, in some instances, looking like a slick lawyer ready for a court appearance. For some mill hands the occasional "full treatment" at Azzie's was his only weekly or monthly indulgence.

The difference in clientele was marked in other ways. Nearly all of Azzie's customers, principally mill workers, used tobacco in one form or another. At times his shop was a stifling haze of cigarette and cigar smoke, so thick and so smelly that it was difficult for the non-smoker to breathe. This was particularly true in the wintertime when it was necessary to keep the shop doors, back and front, closed. However, few complained. Those who didn't smoke usually chewed tobacco or dipped snuff, causing them to expectorate onto the street. This climate of smoke and noise was very different from that at Charley Bell's shop.

It wasn't that patrons at Charley Bell's didn't use tobacco. They did, from the highest to the lowest. The difference lay in the numbers. As noted above, "Old Man Joe" Bridger, president of the Bladenboro Cotton Mills, continued to munch on his tobacco while having his hair clipped, and he didn't hesitate to interrupt Charley Bell and relieve himself of a mouthful of spit on the sidewalk. However, unlike Azzie's place, Charley Bell's shop never seemed to be over-run by a raucous cigarette-smoking, tobacco-chewing crowd of mill hands like that that patronized his competitor. His shop was quieter, more sedate, and the air cleaner.

Male youngsters growing up in Bladenboro progressed from childhood into young adulthood having their hair cut at either Azzie's or Charley Bell's barbershop about every two weeks, that is, unless a parent cut their hair at home, which was often the case. In the thirties, the cost of haircuts was minimal--fifteen cents for a child and a quarter for an adult. Even so, for some potential customers those prices were sufficiently high during the depression to keep them away. Not until the war years did the price began to climb so that by the mid-fifties the standard price for an adult haircut in both shops had moved up to seventy-five cents, still cheap, however, by big-city standards.

Most youngsters in and around Bladenboro visited one of the shops and absorbed the atmosphere and comradery that prevailed in these truly cultural centers. The time they spent there while growing up taught them many things about life, values, community and world events, politics, local gossip, sports, the economy, the living and the dead. Sitting in the shops, particularly Azzie's shop, while the barbers seemingly worked at a snail's pace with hand clippers and scissors and a straight razor was a learning experience where the young and old associated with each other. In the process, youngsters were initiated into the male culture of the town as they waited their turn in the chair. The shops helped one to establish his identity through interaction with others.

Azzie and Charley Bell knew nearly everyone in the southern portion of Bladen County and how they were connected by marriage or blood. Thus they were repositories of local lore, men who made intangible but significant contributions in cementing the town together. They knew you, who your parents were, who your relatives were, and how you fitted into the tangled marital relationships existing among the families that made up the Bladenboro community. They knew stories about your parents and relatives and what their reputations were in the community, whether perceived as being hard workers, honest, religious, or otherwise. They helped youngsters to know who they were and how they fitted into the life of the community. In doing so, they made a visit to their shops a memorable experience.

Chapter 7

A Town of Churches

To live in Bladenboro during the thirties and forties was to live in the shadow of churches. Whatever direction one took from the town's solitary stoplight hanging over the intersection of NC 211 and NC 410 at the center of town, one was certain to soon encounter a house of worship. And on several side roads off these highways near town, the same was true. Within a radius of six to eight miles from the town's center, there were numerous churches that served the religious needs of the local population. Churches were seemingly everywhere. Had it been possible for these edifices to be suddenly removed, the town's structural architecture and its immediate environs would have been radically altered. The presence of so many sanctuaries in such a small area suggested not only great religious diversity of doctrinal belief and ritual, but it also suggested the presence of a people whose character was formed and then guided by profound faith.

Less than a half-mile west of town toward Lumberton on NC 211 were located in close proximity the Church of God and the White Oak Original Free Will Baptist Church, at that time my parents' church. Both the existing church structures had been built new in the forties. However, White Oak was a long established church dating back to the early nineteen hundreds, whereas the Church of God originated there in the forties. Furthermore, located a short distance off this highway on a county road running north through the nearby Old Mill village of the Bladenboro Cotton Mills were the West Bladenboro Missionary

Baptist Church and the Fire Baptized Holiness Church (later renamed the New Light Pentecostal Church). These sanctuaries were on the northern periphery of the mill village commonly called the "old mill hill." Another close-by church west of town on NC 211 was the Bethel Emanuel Holiness Church. It was situated directly across the highway and the Seaboard Airline Railroad from the southeast entrance to the company's New Mill. Because of their proximity to the mills, the membership of these five churches consisted principally of textile workers and their families.

Farther west on NC 211 but less than two miles from town was the Bryant Swamp Baptist Church that served the black community around Richmond. Thus, within a distance of several miles between the town and the Big Swamp, which served as the county line between Bladen and Robeson counties, there were six functioning churches during the thirties and forties. Within recent times, a new sanctuary called the Outreach for Christ Church has been established to the west of town just beyond the Pine Ridge Community and the former site of the now demolished New Mill.

With the exception of the Bryant Swamp Baptist Church that served Richmond's black population, the membership in the other five churches was exclusively white and working-class because the bulk of their membership worked in the nearby cotton mills. For example, my own family with its numerous relatives, principally the descendants of Daniel Edmond and Excie Hester, were mill operatives and made up the majority of members in White Oak Original Free Will Baptist Church. A few congregational members who earned their livelihood from farming and clerking in retail stores–about the only other occupational options to textile work then available–were nearly invisible in the membership. Personal visits to several of the other churches (for example, the West Bladenboro Baptist Church) revealed the same working-class membership. The same individuals whom one might see if entering the mills were the same individuals, if churchgoers, that one might see when visiting these congregations.

From the mills and these churches emerged a number of working-class ministers who felt the "call" to preach. As mentioned earlier, Holland Hughes, Julian Smith, James Hester, Gaston Hester and others are but a few of the men who combined labor in the mills with religious ministry. Their churches provided an outlet for experiences and growth in leadership that these individuals would never have had if not members of their congregations. For most textile workers, their jobs offered few if any opportunities to demonstrate any talent beyond that of tending machines. The churches provided opportunities for the expression of latent leadership talents. Thus the significant number of men called into the ministry from these congregations during this time suggests that stultifying conditions in the workplace combined with a strong evangelistic faith to produce in some a spiritual awakening that made them more sensitive to the "call."

In the center of town on the west side of what was once called Front Street (now Main Street) was the Presbyterian Church. Located less than a block from the stoplight, the church was an old wooden structure that sat on a spacious lot between the Lyric Theater and the Bank of Bladenboro. Directly across Front Street from the church during the Great Depression years was M. Nance's fish and hamburger stand. Even in the decades of the thirties and forties, the ravages of age were evident on the church building and required much maintenance. Its congregation was small and mixed consisting of a few mill hands (such as my Aunts Clara Tyler and Mae McLamb) a few prominent residents of Front Street (such as the Dr. S. S. Hutchinson family) and a few farmers (such as Frank Davis). Consequently, during the fifties a dwindling congregation decided to dispose of the valuable downtown property and to build a much smaller, brick sanctuary on the west side of Front Street across the Seaboard Railroad tracks and beyond the depot and adjacent to the town's Henry Clyde Bridger Library. Much later when the Presbyterian Church ended its services there, the property was acquired by the Calvary Independent Church. My first contact with the old, downtown Presbyterian Church was through Reverend Benjamin Ormand, a wonderful man, who served as bimonthly pastor. He was also the leader of Boy Scout Troop 72 of which I was a member.

Within a block of Calvary Independent on the east side of Front Street was the First Baptist Church whose membership included the most influential people in town. This was the church home of the families that owned the Bladenboro Cotton Mills and other enterprises, the town's merchants, and a few professionals. A beautiful but small brick church, First Baptist was a fitting structure to grace the "Street of Beautiful Homes," as Front Street was locally known. Unlike other sanctuaries in the area, its interior layout was not rectangular but semi-circular, with its curved pews designed to focus downward toward the pulpit and upward toward a small, slightly elevated choir loft to the right. This arrangement created a sense of intimacy among worshipers, ministers, and choir members. Next to the church was a substantial frame parsonage, painted white, with an expansive front porch that faced Front Street. First Baptist was the only local church in the thirties and forties that retained a full-time minister **and** provided him with a parsonage. That it did so was a measure of the relative affluence of its congregation when compared to others in the area. Front Street (NC 410) ran through the heart of Bladenboro past the white elementary and white high schools to the south end of town and on to Chadbourn. However, shortly before reaching the schools, NC 410 was joined by NC 131, a road that linked it to NC 701 that connected Clarkton to Whiteville. During the thirties and forties, no churches existed on NC 131 between Bladenboro and the Bladen-Columbus county line. During the sixties, however, the First Baptist Church established an outreach mission on NC 131 near a water-logged section called Hog Wallow. Sustained by the support of the parent church, in time the mission, a small frame structure, evolved into the independent Grace Baptist Church. And farther down NC 131 near the Bladen-Columbus county line, area residents established the New Center Baptist Church, somewhat larger than Grace Baptist--yet still small--brick sanctuary. It drew its members from the families, like that of my Uncle Woodrow Edwards, living on the rich farmland surrounding the church. Consequently, if one traveled from the single stoplight in downtown Bladenboro south along Front Street and southeast along NC 131 to the county line, a distance of less than five miles, there are now four churches, two of which during the thirties were located within a quarter-mile of each other inside the town limits. As along NC 211 west to the Robeson County line, the religious landscape along NC 131 south to the Columbus County line has changed since the decades of depression and war.

Approximately a mile down NC 410 beyond the Bladenboro High School (now a Middle school) and the Bridger Cemetery (now Pinecrest) toward Chadbourn was another long-standing Baptist church called Galeed. It was situated off the highway from which it could be easily seen by travelers. Although originally a wooden structure during the thirties and forties, Galeed rebuilt in the fifties and is now a lovely brick structure whose members, unlike those in the churches above, maintains a cemetery for its deceased members. Its membership consisted principally of small farmers living in the area and a few mill workers from the Bladenboro Cotton Mills. At the time, Galeed Baptist Church was the only church on NC 410 between Bladenboro and the Columbus County line.

However, on off-roads in the rural area south of town, there were other influential churches such as Lennons' Crossroads Baptist Church and Mount Calvary Original Free Will Baptist Church whose members were mostly farmers who were economically, socially, and educationally linked to the town. For example, many of my mother' family were members of Mount Calvary and my Grandfather Charley Edwards is buried there. My earliest visits to this church was to a wooden structure, but like so many of the sanctuaries of the thirties and forties, it has been replaced with a modern brick structure. Mount Calvary was one of three Original Free Will Baptist churches in the immediate Bladenboro area.

If one traveled eastward from the town's stoplight along NC 211 (now known as Martin Luther King Drive), one went through a racially mixed but principally black settlement that had its own school and its two churches. As noted earlier, this was an era of racial segregation so that the membership of the churches previously discussed was entirely white. Although the black population east of town was not large there were nevertheless two churches existing beside the highway: one was the St. Luke AME Zion Church and the other was the First Baptist Church, which should not be confused with the First Baptist Church of Bladenboro located on Front Street. (Many years later the Front Street First Baptist added "of Bladenboro" to its name in order to distinguish it from its black counterpart on NC 211.) Even though a few whites lived in the immediate area, the congregations of these two churches were entirely black.

For as long as I can remember, St. Luke's was a small wooden structure whose services served black Methodists in the area. In the summer with windows up, its services often produced a joyful worship heard by neighboring households. As mentioned above, my Aunt Clara and her husband once rented a small house adjacent to St. Luke's and as a boy visiting on Sunday evening during the summer, we sat on the front porch while services were underway. Wonderfully enthusiastic music flowed through the open windows of the church. Now when I hear African-American religious groups sing, I always remember those Sunday evening on Aunt Clara's porch listening to those joyous sounds.

Within a short distance but on the opposite side of NC 211 was the First Baptist Church. Like St. Luke, it was located near a row of warehouses where processed cotton was stored, bales that were the product of a nearby cotton gin that processed much of the locally produced cotton that was principally used in the Bladenboro Cotton Mills. While growing up, I never had occasion to learn much about this church even though as a boy I passed it frequently while trying to sell the Grit newspaper and broom-straw brooms in the black community. Other than denominationally–one being Methodist, the other Baptist–I do not know how the black parishioners to the two churches were divided, because other than a few evenings sitting and listening to the enthusiastic services at St. Luke, I have no idea of the numbers attending either church or how they differentiated themselves. I suspect that tradition or religious differences in ideology primarily determined the distribution of black membership.

Immediately north of Bladenboro, NC 410 splits, part angling off toward Dublin and part (NC 242) angling off toward Elizabethtown, the seat of Bladen County. Several miles north on NC 242 is Sandy Grove Baptist Church and its cemetery. In the thirties and forties–and even today–its membership consisted primarily of small farm families who lived in the vicinity of the church. Although on the periphery of Bladenboro, like similar other churches (for example, Mount Calvary) it was near enough to be thought of as part of the town's religious structure. And the same was true of Zion Hill Baptist Church that was located northward on NC 410. Like a lot of the local churches then, Zion Hill Baptist was a wooden structure that was later replaced by a modern brick sanctuary. Its membership consisted of local farm families, a few textile workers (for example, my Uncle Major and Aunt Itus) and others. Somewhat farther to the north and located on a rural road connecting NC 410 and NC 242 was the Oak Grove Original Free Will Baptist Church and its cemetery. It was the third church of this denomination in the Bladenboro area. My mother's people (Edwards and Hesters) had a long-standing connection with Oak Grove Church where Fannie Edwards (my maternal grandmother) and other relatives are buried. Its members, too, then consisted principally of small farm families living in the immediate area. Oak Grove, Sandy Grove, and

Zion Hill, together with other out-of-town churches, such as Galeed Baptist and West Bladenboro Baptist, were located on unpaved roads, roads that were not paved until after World War II.

Although all the above churches continue to exist in and around Bladenboro, there are now many more of different religious hues. Undoubtedly, there are numerous reasons for this proliferation that seems not to be unique to Bladenboro but is countrywide. During the thirties and forties, a common denominator for the Bladenboro churches was that they were–and continue to be–all Protestant. (One will not find a synagogue, a mosque, or a Catholic church in or around the town.) Although with an exception or two all the churches tended to be evangelistic in their approach to worship, their belief systems were remarkably the same. And because of the Great Depression followed by World War II attendance at Sunday church services was undoubtedly substantial. This strong religious commitment continues to undergird not only Bladenboro but all of Bladen County. For example, a reading of the twice-weekly issues of the Bladen Journal reveals a listing of all the county churches, a listing that fills one news page of fine print. Just as one can conclude that the number of churches in the decades of the thirties and forties was evidence of a very religious people inhabiting Bladenboro and its immediate environs, the modern day listing of so many sanctuaries in the Bladen Journal, which includes those in Bladenboro, provides strong evidence of a strong, continuing religious influence throughout the county.

Chapter 8

Early Entertainment in the 'Boro

As a small rural, textile village situated in the backwaters of eastern North Carolina, Bladenboro was not a town where, during the thirties and forties, one expected to find a great variety of sophisticated entertainment. Like many small towns in such out-of-the-way places, the daily east-west movement of passenger and freight trains on the Seaboard tracks often provided the only distraction from life's mundane affairs. Nevertheless, residents of the town, the Old and New mill villages, and the surrounding countryside who flooded its streets on Friday afternoons and Saturdays were often surprised at what awaited them. On these two days, "Going to the 'Boro'" was an absolute, psychic necessity for many, a habitual ritual considered necessary to successfully complete the work week in anticipation of a quiet, peaceful Sunday when little occurred except religious services in area churches. Although the quality of entertainment in Bladenboro during those decades failed miserably to match that enjoyed by its modern-day residents, occasionally out-of-town entertainers arrived, set up shop, and provided milling farmers, mill hands and others alternative opportunities for distraction than the "picture shows" running in W. G. Fussell's Lyric Theater.

Among the earliest forms of transient entertainment that I recall were the medicine shows that came to town in the early thirties and then disappeared forever. As a very small boy, I remember attending three such shows with my father. The first of these performances occurred near the Old Mill village where we then lived. Off highway NC 211 and immediately east of the Seaboard Railroad siding that serviced the Bladenboro Cotton Mills was a beautiful grove of towering, magnificent long-leaf pines located directly behind several mill houses fronting the rail siding. Years later these trees were cut for timber. This grove was then part of the Latt Edwards estate that lay contiguous to mill property. It was here that mill workers often congregated on Sunday afternoon to smoke, chew tobacco, dip snuff, and talk the hours away.

One Saturday morning within an opening on this beautiful pine setting near the highway, the owner of a traveling medicine show set up for business from the back of a good-sized, flat-bed truck, a portion of which was covered, the rest an open stage for addressing potential customers. Of course, his purpose was to sell his bottled medicinal concoctions to anyone foolish enough to buy them. He chose an ideal spot to conduct his business because it was directly across the intersection that joined NC 211 to the principal road leading into the Old Mill village. On Saturdays these roads were used by workers and their families walking en route to and from Bladenboro. They walked because there was no public transportation and very few owned cars. Like their farm counterparts living in the surrounding area, mill people felt a compulsion to spend most of every Saturday whiling away the time in town visiting and shopping for items they could not obtain at the company store. Consequently, the site under the pines chosen by the proprietor of the medicine show was ideally positioned to be seen by and attract a transient audience of mill folk.

En route to Bladenboro from the Old Mill village on that Saturday, my father and I approached a noisy of crowd of thirty or forty men and women gathered around the truck bed. On it sat a slouchily-clad man in a chair strumming a guitar and singing. Out of curiosity, my father and I joined the expectant crowd. As it turned out, the man with the guitar was the "show." His picking and singing did little to reduce the noisy chatter of the people gathered there, most of them mill workers who were a naturally talkative lot. Faced with an inattentive and unappreciative audience, the musical "entertainment" did not last long. When it ended, a second man, dressed in rumpled clothing and looking little better than the guitar player, came out from the covered part of the truck bed and began to hawk his medicinal products. I don't remember any of his comments about the effectiveness of his medicines, but my Uncle

Major, Dad's brother who was in the crowd, was persuaded to buy a bottle of the elixir perhaps in the hope of "curing" whatever unknown problem he had. Later, my father joked with him about the "snake oil" medicine he had purchased and about his foolishness in believing what the salesman had said about its curative powers. The patent medicine, I suppose, had been presented as a panacea, a "cure all," for the aches and pains that mill folk complained about–and there were many bona fide complaints that resulted from work in the hot and lint-filled mills. As I recall, there was a brisk sale of the hawker's bottles, some folks buying it as much out of curiosity as a conviction that it would ease their aches and pains. In any case, the "show" helped to break the monotony of mill and village life.

I recall two other medicine shows that my father and I briefly attended. One evening just before dark, we were returning from town en route back to the Old Mill village along NC 211 when we came across another crowd gathered in a field that lay between A. C. Hardin's small store and Caz Deavers' work shed. In the thirties, a gathering crowd in Bladenboro always indicated that something interesting was occurring. In this case, it was another hawker making every effort to convince his listeners about the curative powers of his patent "medicines." After my father had spoken to several people, we left the milling crowd that was spilling over onto the highway and creating hazardous road conditions. We didn't stay long enough to discover the nature of the "show," nor do I remember hearing anyone discuss it, but some form of entertainment was always part of the "medicine show" experience. On another day, either before or after this episode, my father and I visited relatives who lived on the Dublin road. On our return–walking, of course–we found a large crowd gathered on high ground under several large trees located near town. Apparently, the entertainment phase was over and done with because the sale of "medicines" was already underway with all faces turned toward the hawker. Again, we spent little time there, simply walking up to the event, speaking to a few people in the crowd, and then promptly leaving. After this event, if there was ever another "medicine show" that found its way into Bladenboro, I was never aware of it.

Before there developed a sensitivity to and a legal prohibition against disparaging people who had developed or been born with grotesque physical deformities, nearly every traveling circus or fair would showcase such folks for pay in so-called "freak" shows. For example, such individuals as a "bearded lady," an "elephant man," a "contortionist," an excessively overweight person, or an individual missing several limbs was inevitably a part of these events. However, in the off season, when the circuses wintered somewhere in a warm climate, some of these individuals would become entrepreneurs and set up shop in small towns like Bladenboro and charge a small admission to be seen. On Saturdays, the streets of Bladenboro was always thronged with people from the farms and mill villages, some of whom were not reluctant to pay a dime for a brief view of, say, the "elephant man." Often these small-time entrepreneurs were not humans displaying themselves. Some of them might hawk an unusual, "one-of-a-kind" animal, for example, the "world's largest rattle snake."

There were several instances that I remember of performances by visiting "oddities," as such people and animals were then often called. For example, next door to Allie Page's restaurant, which at one time had been the lobby of a now defunct hotel in the Hutchinson block, an "elephant man" set up shop one Saturday afternoon and charged customers a dime for a quick view of his hardened elephant-like skin. Advertising was by word of mouth. I don't know what his customers expected to see, perhaps a man with a huge, trunk-like nose, but I recall hearing some disappointed viewers complain that the spectacle was not gruesome or exciting enough for the dime they had paid. And on another Saturday in the same location, I recall that someone had on display a "two-headed" animal of some sort, which I was unable to view because I lacked the dime admission. Perhaps it was just as well, because several friends who saw the "two-headed" thing came out of the exhibit disgusted, claiming it was all a fake and bemoaning the loss of their money. Events like these would not occur today, but in the thirties and early forties they added a little spice to the lives of people beset by depression and hard work on the farms and in the mills.

During the thirties, the streets of Bladenboro on Saturdays were always interesting. M. Nance (I never learned what the M. stood for.) and his wife ran a hamburger stand located between Vaught's Cash Store and a small wooden Savings & Loan building managed by Theron Pait. In the absence of an eating establishment other than the Page restaurant, where most locals were reluctant to inter and probably because it catered to the "better" element of the town, M's stand was usually the gathering place for street people desiring food. Although M. and his wife were notorious snuff and tobacco users even while preparing food, they nevertheless sold delicious hamburgers, hot dogs, fish sandwiches, and cold drinks to inside and outside customers. Around noon time, there usually was a mob of people patronizing the business. And sometimes, interesting and entertaining events occurred while people milled around eating and talking in the empty space that separated M.'s stand from the Savings & Loan business. For example, one Saturday someone parked a flat-bed truck in the empty space and when the crowd was thickest, a young girl came out in Shirley Temple fashion and began to dance about on the trailer bed. Her father was selling a product of some sort and was using his daughter to focus the milling crowd on his spiel. I can't recall what the response of the crowd was to his efforts, nor do I remember the specific product. (On Saturdays, individuals were constantly selling various items on the streets of Bladenboro. At one time, even I sold bags of "salty-boiled" peanuts for a nickel a bag, attempted to shine shoes until my mother found out about my enterprise, and sold limited copies of the Grit newspaper.) The young, dancing girl caused the mob to gather, many of them eating one of M's hamburgers and drinking a cold Coke or Pepsi from his ice box, their lunch for the day.

That same location was also the site for fledgling street preachers. With all the farmers and mill people in town, the throng in the street was a ready-built congregation for spreading the Word. Some beginning preachers used the ever-changing crowd to hone their message of the Gospel, and they always attracted the more religious elements who were in town to buy the week's groceries or to conduct other business. They also attracted the curious who stopped for a few moments and moved on. There were not many of these preachers who converted the street around M.'s hamburger stand into a pulpit, but I do remember that the preaching of those who did was marked by great enthusiasm and energy. For many in the crowd who stopped to listen, the sermon was just a distraction from their business in town, but others took the service very seriously. But for most, however, the impromptu service probably helped to while away the time while consuming one of M.'s juicy hamburgers. As for M., I suspect that he viewed these sporadic outbursts of street preaching as good for business.

Throughout the thirties, the nation was beset by a host of highly publicized hoodlums, especially bootleggers and bank robbers. The general public was fascinated and intrigued by these gangsters, some of whom became popular heroes. Men like Pretty Boy Floyd, Machine Gun Kelly, Baby Face Nelson, John Dillinger, Al Capone–all had a reputation for mayhem and violence that reached every small town and village and helped to divert people's attention away from the economic woes of the times. Of course, although the people of Bladenboro were then in the backwash of southeastern North Carolina, they were not ignorant of these villains. The notorious deeds of these men seemed to be known to most of the young boys who were my friends. Consequently, it was not surprising that small-time entrepreneurs should exploit the dramatic, lawless deeds of these men for profit.

Once on a summer Saturday afternoon, one of these businessmen set up a small tent near Arthur Waterson's filling station (now gone) on a site where after World War II Dr. Sankey S. Hutchinson would build a back-door addition to his drugstore and medical office. Perhaps anticipating Madame Toussaud's wax museum of renowned personalities in London, the transient entrepreneur had created the likenesses of about a half-dozen of the decade's most notorious outlaws in menacing postures, some of whom were still being sought by the FBI and the state police for bank robbery, murder, and other crimes. With the payment of a dime, one was allowed to go inside the tent and spend a few moments of make believe with these artful, true-to-life creations as the owner told about their exploits. The exhibit attracted a number of youngsters, including myself, who had learned about the criminals portrayed in wax by means of Saturday newsreels at W. G. Fussel's Lyric Theater and perhaps the radio, if one's family was fortunate enough to have one. As I recall, there were no counterparts to the likenesses of these gangsters, that is, there was no portrayal of the lawmen who sought to track down these public enemies. After the exhibit moved on, for awhile the game of cowboys and Indians, which was the principal game played among young boys, was sometimes cast aside in favor of cops and robbers, at least until memory either faded of the exhibit or was pushed aside by the stream of Saturday western movies shown at the Lyric Theater.

Of course, the Lyric Theater was the principal source of entertainment for most of the people who crowded the streets of Bladenboro on Saturdays, that is, except for those persons who did not have the admission price and those whose religious beliefs had convinced them that all movies were downright evil and sinful and should be avoided at all costs. Unfortunately, for some the prevailing hard times of the thirties made every penny essential for necessities and their money could not be wasted on frivolous "picture shows." When Fussel agreed to accept in lieu of cash–at a premium, of course–the fiat coins of the Bladenboro Cotton Mills, commonly known as "Maggie's Gold," many hard pressed workers found it even more difficult to attend the movies because the premium made the price of admission even more expensive for them.

Furthermore, for most members of local evangelical churches, hard-nosed religious beliefs concerning sin, hellfire, and damnation prevented them from enjoying the Saturday fare at the Lyric Theater, or, the Wednesday night movie, or, the so-called "Owl Show" at midnight on Saturday night. For them movie going was only one of a multitude of sins that included wearing jewelry, dancing, playing cards, swearing, drinking–even soft drinks such as Coca Cola or Pepsi Cola–anyone of which, if indulged in, could send one's soul to an everlasting hell. Consequently, such members of these denominations steered clear of the Lyric Theater rather than risk being eternally lost. Nevertheless, there were a few members who saw little harm or no harm in the "shows" at the Lyric and attended even though in doing so they risked being expelled from their congregations for their sinful lifestyle.

It is now difficult to comprehend that anyone would see soul-searing harm in the kinds of movies shown at the Lyric Theater. Except for the "Owl Show" that began Saturday at midnight, which usually featured a spooky, scary show of some sort (for example, Frankenstein), the Saturday feature was always a western, a serial, and a comedy. Saturday after Saturday, either Roy Rogers, Gene Autry, Ken Maynard, Buck Jones, Lash Larue, Text Ritter, Bob Steele and others tore across the screen fighting the bad guys, upholding law and order, and protecting the weak and innocent. The format for these westerns was always the same, so much so that one could stand outside the theater and know what action was underway on the screen from the music spilling out into the street. After the action-packed feature came an equally thrilling–and harmless–serial, usually something like Flash Gordon or Zorro–each episode always ending in such a way as to entice one back for the next. And always there was a comedy to top off the entertainment that usually featured comics like the Three Stooges, Ed Wynn, or Andy Clyde. For the price–usually ten cents for children under twelve or a quarter for adults–one could spend a couple of hours in make believe that helped to while away a Saturday afternoon. For those persons with time and money, the Lyric Theater offered a Wednesday night showing that included the major releases from Hollywood.

But it was the Saturday offering at the Lyric that was attended by most locals, especially youngsters, some of whom daringly violated their parents' instructions never to attend this den of iniquity. One could enter the theater at any time (for example, in the middle of the feature) and remain there as long as one wanted, even to spending the entire afternoon watching the offering over and over until forced to leave by parents. Unlike modern theaters where refreshments are often more expensive than the price of admission, the Lyric sold cheap popcorn and sodas. With an extra nickel or dime, youngsters could feast off these goodies while totally absorbed in watching the exciting action on the screen. Often filled with children, the Lyric was a noisy place on Saturday afternoon, not only because Roy or Gene were either fighting or shooting up the bad guys when not singing love songs to the heroine, but also because of the loud, unrestrained talking and yakking of youngsters. For them the westerns later became the basis of cowboy and Indian play with pretend "gangs" and their posse pursuers roaming over Bryant Swamp in search of each other. Fussell's Lyric Theater helped to enliven what might have been dull Saturday afternoons as well as stimulated childhood play throughout the summer weeks when school was not in session. It goes without saying that adult patrons also immensely enjoyed the temporary diversions from the difficult times that the Lyric Theater provided.

Another sporadic form of entertainment that locals around Bladenboro enjoyed during the thirties and forties was the "fair," a term widely used to cover a variety of traveling amusements. Unlike today when the term principally applies to county and state fairs with exhibits (especially livestock and other agricultural products), special events of all kinds (such as horse and sulky racing, live musical entertainment), and a dozen kinds of rides and food kiosks, fairs held in Bladenboro were more limited in what they offered to those who ventured out to visit them. Generally, they were not events that provided lasting memories. However, although there was nothing to set them apart, while growing up I do recall four "fairs" that came to town.

The first of these occurred when I was a small boy, and it would not remotely fit the modern definition of a fair. Near the same towering long-leaf pines where I saw a medicine show, a small-time operator set up a two-piece amusement center that consisted of swings and a carousel or, as we called it then, a merry-go-round. When attending modern day fairs, I don't see swings of the same type that then attracted so many dare-devil teenagers from the nearby mill villages and town. With bucket seats attached to chains suspended from a raised rotating wheel powered by a gasoline engine, patrons with enough courage–or stupidity–to risk life and limb tightly gripped the chains as the wheel turned faster and faster forcing the riders higher and higher off the ground. It was a dangerous ride because of the tremendous centrifugal force built up in the circular swing. There were reported instances in which broken chains or loosed bolts on such devices resulted in fatalities. Unlike today, there were no safety regulations or inspections of the swings to guarantee that accidents did not happen. One enjoyed such rides at one's own risk. However, the carousel with its hobby horses was safe. (Perhaps more dangerous than either ride was the occasional car that raced by on NC 211 and endangered the milling crowd that often spilled out onto the road.) This road between the New Mill village and Bladenboro was already a death trap without having careless fair-goers carelessly wandering onto its lanes. As I recall, within a decade at least five young people had been killed by cars on that short stretch of road.

On another occasion, a circus came to town and set up east of the Bridger Corporation store and Henry White's livery stables facing the Seaboard Railroad. Even though a small boy at the time, I remember the event very well because Aunt Clara and Uncle D. Tyler took me there. It was my first experience at seeing live circus animals like elephants and even under a big tent. It was a wonderful event for a small boy like myself. Later when a teenager, there was a similar circus that opened near the Old Mill village on an empty lot behind the Latt Edwards old home place. This was a memorable occasion because an elephant temporarily escaped and its trainer had trouble reasserting control over the animal. A high-school friend name Dewey Russ, who at the time was slightly inebriated, showed remarkable courage by threatening to break off the elephant's "snout" if it approached the bed of the pickup truck where he was standing. Fortunately, the trainer "captured" the elephant before Dewey did major damage to its trunk.

There were other so-called fairs over the years on locations around Bladenboro. One such site was the ballpark next to the high school which once was surrounded by a wooden fence and grandstand. Unfortunately, in 1943 these burned together with the adjacent school gymnasium that had been built by WPA/PWA during the depression of the thirties. What remained was on open space for a ball diamond and a football field. Of course, in the late summer when not being used by the schools athletic teams, the open field was an excellent site for traveling rides and entertainment booths. Sometime during the mid- or-late forties, shortly after World War II, a small company set up rides there that included a ferris wheel, a carousel, swings, and booths where one could lose money in a variety of ways, for example, by throwing darts at balloons and baseballs at targets for cheap stuffed animals, and tossing coins at bottle tops that represented a mild form of gambling. As I recall, when visiting the event, there was never a large crowd, either in the afternoon or evening openings. With the exception of young people who may have gone in order to have something to do, the patrons appeared to be individuals who visited out of curiosity, not to spend money on entertainment. After Saturday night's business, the rides and booths were quickly disassembled, loaded on trucks and rapidly disappeared into the night to set up in another town.

A similar, although smaller company, set up for business in a vacant lot near Grover Pait's trucking firm east of town off NC 211. Its rides were limited to swings and a carousel. I was fortunate in that I hired on as a ticket seller for the swings, making the grand sum of ten cents an hour for my labor. Another friend sold tickets to the carousel. The visit of these traveling fairs were very infrequent. The swings and carousel stayed for one week before the owner dismantled the rides and moved on. This and other so-called "fairs" added little to the culture of entertainment in Bladenboro; however, their occasional visits did add a bit of variety to life in this small town.

Perhaps the most popular form of entertainment occurred during the summer when the ball club of the Bladenboro Cotton Mills began to play its schedule in a developing textile league. The games were originally played in an open field between the Seaboard Railroad and the residence of Jarvis Davis whose occupation was installing fresh water hand pumps. The field was close to the Old Mill, the company store, and the two mill villages, making the games easily accessible to scores of people who worked, traded, and lived there. The games were usually played on Saturday afternoons when most mill operatives were off work for the weekend. Later on the games were moved to the Bladenboro High School ballpark south of town. As noted above, prior to its fiery destruction the park was enclosed with a wooden, slat fence. Furthermore, the fans were able to sit in stands with an overhang that protected them from both sun and rain. I remember attending games there and hearing the unique noise caused by the crack of wooden bats slamming against baseballs, a sound that echoed throughout the enclosure. It was a wonderful sound! Unfortunately, in 1943 when many of the young players were in military service, the stands, the fence, and the school gymnasium burned, leaving an open field.

After World War II, the Bladenboro Cotton Mills built an excellent ball facility with stands northwest of town near the New Mill village for the "Spinners" (the name given the ball club). Everyone in Bladenboro–not just mill workers and their families–took a special interest and pride in the Spinners because its players, with a few exceptions, consisted of young men who worked in the mills and several sons of prominent families in town. In the summertime, local baseball was truly a major form of local entertainment, reflecting, of course, the general, nationwide interest in baseball as a past-time. When not watching the local team, many residents of Bladenboro followed radio broadcasts of their favorite major league teams. It was not uncommon for broadcasts of these games to attract a crowd to the front porch of a mill villager who was fortunate enough to have a radio and was willing to share the broadcasts with his neighbors.

In addition to the forms of entertainment noted above, activities at the local school provided many people of Bladenboro with diversions in their lives. Prior to the war, school sports always attracted members of the community who enjoyed watching the Bladenboro Bulldogs play competitors in football, baseball, and boys and girls basketball. However, these sports were interrupted by the war and were not revived until the Fall of 1945 when once again they became part of school and community life. Once again sports combined with school and community play productions to provide entertainment for some. Apart from sports, young people entertained themselves in a variety of ways–private parties that often features games like spin-the-bottle and postoffice, school sponsored socials, and peanut boilings. Of course, such activities were not part of the public entertainment that was part of the life of Bladenboro.

Chapter 9

Boy Scouts–Troop 72

Although not a major institution in Bladenboro, the Boy Scout troop that the local Rotary Club sponsored in the early forties greatly impacted the lives of teenagers who lived close enough to town to participate. The formation of Troop 72 provided numerous opportunities for wholesome activities for local boys at a time when the world was being torn apart by a destructive war in which most of them were destined to be drafted and fed into the nation's war machine. Knowing the probable fate of the town's young males, the likely intent of Rotary Club members (a few of whom were veterans of World War I) in sponsoring the troop was to introduce the local boys to some aspects and practices of military life that they were likely to encounter when eventually entering active service. However, undoubtedly there were other motives. Whatever the motivation of the sponsors, membership in the troop turned out to be a very positive experience for the dozen or so boys who participated.

The man selected as the scoutmaster was Reverend Benjamin Ormand. Reverend Ormand was a minister who served the now demolished Presbyterian Church that was located on Front (now Main) Street diagonally across the street from Vaught's Cash Store and M. Nance's hamburger stand. There were not many Presbyterians in Bladenboro, certainly not enough to support a resident, full-time minister and parsonage as did the more numerous and prominent Baptists in town. Nevertheless, this small Presbyterian congregation did include several prominent families, for example, that of Dr. S. S.

Hutchinson, Frank Davis, and Foster Davis, and others, who were committed to continuing services in their faith. Consequently, in lieu of a full-time pastor the congregation opted to have bi-monthly preaching services. This was not an unusual practice for small congregations during the thirties and forties when times were hard and money scarce. It was because of this situation that Reverend Ornand, who lived elsewhere, came to Bladenboro periodically as both minister and scoutmaster.

How the leaders of the Rotary Club came to select Reverend Ormand as scoutmaster and whether compensation was involved are unknown to me. I don't recall that there were any boys in the troop who attended the Presbyterian Church, which, had there been, perhaps would have been reason enough for the reverend's willingness to lead the troop. Even if not, it was evident that he enjoyed working with young boys regardless of their religious affiliation. His choice to lead the newly formed troop was certainly a good choice. A man in his mid-thirties or early forties and about average height, he was somewhat fleshy, although not overweight, and certainly not a softie. He had no reluctance about camping out with his scouts without the usual camping equipment that was unavailable because of prevailing wartime scarcities–no tents, no fancy cooking equipment, no gas lanterns, and so on. His willingness to rough it outdoors with members of the troop and the early rapport that he established with us led to our liking and respecting him as both a scoutmaster and minister. He led by example and personified the Scout Oath and Scout Laws. Without a doubt, he was an extremely positive influence on the boys in Troop 72 whom he led as scoutmaster until reassigned in his pastoral duties.

Since its founding, the outdoors life has been the major focus of the Boy Scout organization and that was certainly true of Troop 72. Furthermore, because the nation was then involved in a world-wide war, there was an increased tendency to focus on camping skills, survival skills, physical fitness, and so on–in other words, any skills that might carry over into military service. In one of the early meetings following my joining upon reaching the age of twelve, Levi Bridger, Sr., who headed the Bank of Bladenboro and who had been a junior army officer during the First World War, attempted to teach the local scouts some of the basic rudiments of military life, such as the commands of "left face," "right face," and "about face" and how to respond to these commands. As I recall, the scouts once assembled on a dimly-lit Front Street where we were instructed in marching commands, such as "forward, march," "to the rear, march," and "oblique, march" and how to respond to these commands. And there were instructions about how to stand in formation. I am not certain Bridger accomplished all he hoped to accomplish with a group of young boys who did not take his drill instructions in the Women's Club House, where the scouts held their meetings, and his marching instructions on Front Street as seriously as they ought, but for some of us who later experienced military service his earlier instructions were not entirely forgotten.

There were other scouting activities where a slightly changed focus was evidently the result of the nation's involvement in a major war. For example, swimming had always been a trade-mark activity of scouts, particularly while camping. For a variety of reasons–health, fitness, safety, rescue–every scout was expected to be a proficient swimmer. However, a new wrinkle to swimming was added that had a military carryover. Whether this minor change was the result of an official Boy Scout directive or simply a change that occurred within the district is unknown. Nevertheless, as I recall, our conversations concerning swimming more and more included reference to "silent swimming" and how to do it, that is, the ability to make a water approach to an enemy person or enemy area as quietly as possible in order to maximize whatever damage we intended to wreak. Other than the pervasive awareness among us of the war, what stimulated such conversations escapes me. I don't recall that Reverend Ormand or any member of the local Rotary Club ever discussed this subject. Nor do I remember any direct instructions given by any adult concerning "silent swimming."

I can remember only one other activity that might be related at least tangentially to the on-going war. In one of our sessions, Rev. Ormand focused on the ability to memorize detailed observations that we made. For example, to develop our ability to retain and reproduce information, he suggested that we study intently the displays in store windows and then try to remember in detail the items observed, the positional relationships of the items to each other, the characteristics of the individual items such as color, the number of items, and so on. It was an exercise that was more difficult than I expected. Oddly enough, I don't remember that the members of Troop 72 spent much time on this subject in subsequent meetings in the Women's Club House.

Reverend Ormand did not appear to be a man who frequently engaged in hard physical work. However, he did believe in physical fitness, which, of course, was part of the Scout Oath. I don't think that his commitment to fitness had anything to do with the on-going war. On the contrary, I think that a healthy body and mind were called for not only in the Scout Oath but also dictated by his Christian beliefs. Consequently, he encouraged troop members to hike, camp, swim, and other activities that helped to create healthy bodies. I can recall only one episode in which he engaged in a physical activity that had overtones of violence and a remote linkage to the military.

It was a practice of the various local Boy Scout troops in the area to hold "camporees" where scouts from various troops joined together in a kind of camping extravaganza to hone up on skills used in outdoor life, such as swimming, knot tying, proper use of hatchets and axes, use of the compass, and survival skills. On one such occasion, a group of scouts sat around a breakfast fire discussing boxing, which was a sport that together with baseball then dominated national radio attention. Reverend Ormand arrived and became part of the discussion about the art of self-defense. Realizing that some of the younger scouts were not familiar with some of the terminology being using by the older boys concerning the techniques of boxing, he offered to give us a demonstration of the pugilistic moves, for example, the jab, the right cross, and the upper cut. He eventually asked one of the larger boys, a tall, rangy fellow from another troop, to join him in the demonstration, a boy who proved very reluctant to strike the minister. Exasperated that the boy's reluctance was making his demonstration of self-defense ineffective, Reverend Ormand shouted to him, "Hit me! Hit me! Don't be afraid, hit me!" Suddenly, the boy slammed a hard right into Reverend Ormand's chest and knocked him flat on his backside. The minister and the scout were embarrassed by the turn of events but each took in all in good humor. However, the blow ended the demonstration.

In addition to the several "camporees" that Troop 72 attended with other area troops, there were numerous weekend camping excursions that occurred because a principal focus of the Boy Scouts is outdoor life. There were several local sites that offered numerous opportunities for tenting, fishing, swimming, hiking and other activities that were essential to scouting. One of the most frequently used camping sites was Bridger's millpond located several miles out of town that Dr. Dewey

H. Bridger made available. The property had a substantial "club house" facing the pond with cooking facilities, a large interior room with tables and chairs, and a large fireplace at its end–a really nice place in a setting of pines. On one occasion, the members of Troop 72 prepared a meal of fish and fish stew for the men of the Rotary Club who wished to attend. But, ordinarily, our activities were outside the club house where we camped under the pines often without tents or sleeping bags because in wartime, these items were hard to acquire. The same was true for the Scout's official uniforms that were just not available. I don't recall any member of the troop having any part of the uniform other than a neckerchief and merit badge sash.

Usually the ones who participated in the camping trips to Bridger's millpond hiked the distance. From the Women's Clubhouse in Bladenboro, there were several approaches to the pond, either of which usually took approximately an hour to two hours to arrive. The seasons did not seem to matter to Rev. Ormand, for I remember camping out on some very cold, clear, starry nights and lying awake while watching meteorites streak across the sky. It was a beautiful site for camping. Sometimes when Rev. Ormand's ministerial responsibilities preventing his coming to Bladenboro for the troop's regular activities, several of us (for example, Sydney Edwards and J. C. Bennett) would hike out and spend the night at the pond. Camping out was one activity that most of us enjoyed. And Bridger's millpond was one of the best that we visited.

Of course, there were other places we used. There were times when we spent a weekend at June Singletary's millpond several miles north of town. During the war years, the pond was a favorite swimming place for boys, especially in the deep cool waters of a pool that lay behind the dam and the relics of an old mill. For those of us fortunate enough to have bicycles a swim in the pond justified the long ride from Bladenboro. Our troop camped out there occasionally, setting up camp beside a small stream that flowed into the pool. On these trips, some of the local men would drive us out and drop us off at the pond and return later to take us back into town. While there we enjoyed swimming and fishing and the comradery of being together. Another site that we occasionally used was Lake Waccamaw. During the forties, Lake Waccamaw was not nearly developed as it is now. We camped at the end of a road running along the lake past an entertainment center then known as the Anchorage. As I recall, the troop spent at least two weekends camping out at the lake. Located miles from Bladenboro, it was necessary for our troops to be transported to Lake Waccamaw. After throwing our gear on the back of a truck provided by a local businessman, about eight or ten of us climbed in behind our goods and rode to the campsite. On one occasion while there, we attended a local church for the military funeral of a submariner who had been killed in action. However, most of our time was spent in the water learning different strokes and water safety, learning about knots, and learning how safely to use hatchets and axes. As I recall, on one occasion the person responsible for returning us to Bladenboro forgot to pick us up. His failure necessitated a long hike to the Anchorage and a long-distanced telephone call to remind him that we were stranded.

Scouting offered opportunities that a few of us took advantage of. For example, there was a Boy Scout camp located at White Lake called Camp Chickagami where scouts could go and spend a week. Some of the Rotarians sponsoring the troop offered to pay the expense of any scout who wished to attend the camp for a week. I took advantage of the offer when Bill Hussey, a man in whose store I worked on the weekends, paid my expenses there. It was a wonderful week. The accommodations were somewhat rickety by today's standards (for example, bunks were of canvas and the huts were primitive) and the food was not the greatest. However, it was wartime and rationing of essential items such as food was a national policy. Therefore, obtaining rationed food for a large bunch of boys–or any other group–was difficult. Consequently, at nearly every noon meal the kitchen served available sour kraut and wieners, a practice that ended forever my eating this dish. Even so, it was a memorable week for meeting new boys and counselors, working on merit badges, hiking (for example, a fourteen-mile hike, there and back, to Singletary Lake), and swimming in the clear waters of White Lake.

Later when I was older, for several weeks during the summer of 1945 I became a counselor at an extremely well-run Boy Scout camp at Singletary Lake that was located seven-miles east of White Lake. The well-constructed camp was formerly a Civilian Conservation Corps (CCC) facility that housed and employed hundreds of local young men during the depression of the thirties and early forties. With about a dozen cabins, a boat house, an extended pier with canoe and boat slips on the lake, a forested environment, and a well-equipped kitchen and dining hall, the former CCC camp was ideal for an extended summer camp for the district's Boy Scouts. Upon arrival, the camp director placed me in charge of a cabin of ten younger boys. During the day, I worked on the waterfront teaching youngsters to swim and to row with oars. It turned out to be a great experience for me, one that I would not have had had I not been involved in scouting. While there, I became a member of the Order of the Arrow and completed several merit badges beyond the Life rank. My experience in scouting was positive. My only regret is that I failed to earn three merit badges shy of reaching Eagle rank.

Unfortunately, with the leaving of Rev. Ormand Troop 72 gradually faded. During the short time that it existed as a minor institution in Bladenboro, it did not impact on the town like some of the others already mentioned. However for the ten or twelve young men who became involved, the experience was very helpful because most of us eventually served in a branch of the military–young men like W. D. Shipman, Harold Bullard, Charles Bridger, Harold White, Richard Pait, J. C. Bennett, Sydney Edwards, Mack Duvall, myself, and others. Furthermore, we were aided by some of the leading men and women of the town who took great interest in the troop–men like Charles Hasbrook, Levi Bridger, Dr. Dewey H. Bridger, Bill and Charles Hussey, other Rotarians, and members of the Women's Club who made their clubhouse available for meetings. They supported the scouts with their time, resources, and expertise, especially assisting in a scout's fulfilling the requirements for merit badges. In a period of great upheaval produced by a destructive, international war, Troop 72 gave a number of young boys in Bladenboro and surrounding area a positive outlet in troubled times.

Chapter 10

Pelo's Pool Emporium

If there was a place in Bladenboro during the thirties and forties that respectable citizens shunned and rejected as a den of iniquity, it was the local pool room situated between Azzie Hardin's barbershop and Searles' five-and-dime store on Highway 211. At a time when ministers and most members of the local churches loudly condemned and railed against drinking, gambling, cursing, fighting, dancing, and even attending movies, the pool room stood foremost as the place in town where the devil was most likely to seduce a young man into a way of life that led straight to hellfire and damnation. Neither "respectable" people nor their children often ventured there because most of the evils noted above were thought to lurk seductively among the racks of cue sticks and the three pool tables, ready to pounce on any innocent who ventured into this Satan's lair. Consequently, most mothers and fathers warned their young sons to avoid the pool room at all costs because of its grave dangers to their immortal souls. These parental instructions were usually accompanied by threats of the dire consequences that would immediately follow if they were disobeyed.

There were good reasons behind the concerns of parents about the town's pool room. It was not uncommon for fights to erupt between players whose consumption of alcohol sometimes caused minor disagreements to escalate into nasty brawls. Furthermore, there was plenty of cheap bootleg whiskey and wine available in the surrounding countryside and, consequently, on the weekends when seemingly everyone came to town, the arrest rate for public intoxication and brawling surged, so much so that the small jail across Highway 211 immediately behind Bill Hussey's store was often filled with drunken, howling prisoners. Because some people who patronized the pool room were inclined to "take a drink" and get "liquored up" a bit before coming to town, it was not uncommon for some of these arrests to be made in the local pool room.

At times, arresting and securing a prisoner in the pool hall was extremely risky business because drunks had a tendency to use their cue sticks as a weapon. Handcuffing and jailing an unruly patron, especially one who might come from a prominent family, was dangerous for the arresting officer who, in Bladenboro, had to be sensitive to the identities of the troublemakers. Yet, in some arrests, more force was used than was absolutely necessary.

Most everyone in town had heard the story of how the local sheriff, had once subdued a young man in the pool hall. Following an encounter between the two men over the sheriff's earlier shooting of a brother that led to an arrest, the young man suddenly broken loose and knocked out a front tooth of the sheriff who swore that in any future encounter with his captive, he would take all appropriate measures to prevent another personal injury. Afterwards when he again found him slightly tipsy and rowdy in the pool hall, without hesitation he viciously assaulted him, beating him mercilessly on the head with his blackjack. The result was devastating. The young man was never quite the same again. The sheriff had subdued his man but at a terrible cost. The story of this violent episode was part of the lore surrounding the pool room, an example told by some parents (for example, my parents) to their children to demonstrate the terrible things that could happen to an innocent young man who ventured into this devil's nest where drinking and gambling were thought to be prevalent.

Unfortunately, portraying the pool hall as an evil and sinister place served to make it even more attractive to many teenage boys growing up in Bladenboro. It was the one place in town where some of the sinful and delightful excesses of adulthood could be daringly observed or indulged, although, of course, at the risk to one's reputation. For one never knew when his presence there might be discovered and reported to parents by a passing neighbor or some town busybody. Nevertheless, like a magnet tugging at iron filings, the forbidden pleasures of the pool hall tugged at a youngster's psyche. Sooner or later, with fear and trembling nearly every teenage male of Bladenboro ventured into the pool hall to indulge in the wicked pleasures thought to reside there.

During the forties, the local pool room was operated by Pelo Lockamy who, like Azzie Hardin, rented his place of business from James A. Bridger. Painted in large block letters across the dingy plate glass windows on either side of the entrance was **PELO'S POOL ROOM**. The chest-high yellow lettering that swept in a semi-circle across the glass immediately caught the eye of curious teenage males who longed to enter. To paint the name of his business, Pelo (everybody called Lockamy, Pelo) most likely had engaged Dick Hilburn, a talented but legless, one-armed painter. Hilburn, who had unfortunately been born without three of his limbs, usually spent the winter months traveling with a circus as part of its freak exhibit. However, while in Bladenboro, he zipped easily about town on a skateboard, using his muscular arm to push himself over the sidewalks. Hilburn employed his considerable artistic talent to paint the names of businesses on the sides of truck cabs for Grover Pait and Carey Dowless, on plate glass windows for customers like Pelo, and to produce picturesque booklets for sale to willing customers wherever found. When painting cabs or store windows, with a powerful thrust of his single arm he hurled his legless body onto a small platform from which he worked.

At the rear of Pelo's long, rectangular pool room was a back door from which one might stand and view a frequently flooded Bryant Swamp that lay directly behind the building. This door was rarely used because it opened out onto the undeveloped edge of the swamp and to piles of trash that had accumulated behind the building. At the rear of the pool room was an enclosed toilet, often stopped up and non-functioning, which emitted all the odors one might expect from such a frequently used but defective facility. Pelo's place was dimly illuminated by reflector lights at the end of drop-cords suspended over the tables from the grooved ceiling. There were three regular sized tables covered in green felt resting on a wooden floor, each with its own ball rack and chalk for the cue tips. On one wall across from the tables, there hung three cue racks, one for each table, with cue sticks of varying lengths and weights to meet the needs of the customers. Along the walls were worn chairs and rough benches for the patrons who sat, smoked, chewed, spat, and talked while waiting impatiently and uncomfortably for a table to open. Pelo's place was not designed for comfort or esthetics. One's only reason for visiting there was to play pool and/or to enjoy the forbidden, risque character of its culture. Otherwise, it was not a place for pleasurable loitering.

During the week when few people had business in town, Pelo's pool room was a relatively quiet place, leaving Pelo plenty of time to stand in the door, smoke, and watch the world go by. As a rule, few individuals ever went into Bladenboro solely to play pool. Nevertheless, on some Wednesday afternoons young, single mill hands coming off the first shift at two o'clock occasionally wandered into town for an evening movie and, while waiting for the "show" to begin, gravitated to Pelo's place. And a few of the more daring high school students sometimes dropped in for a game while en route home, or perhaps spent an afternoon playing hooky there. This was the time of week when novices had sufficient time to hone their skill because there was no pressure to get on with a game and open up the table for waiting customers. In contrast, the weekends at Pelo's were very different because nearly everyone within miles poured into town to shop, to see a movie at W. G. Fussell's Lyric (later the Wonet) Theater, to get a haircut at Azzie's or Charley Bell's, to buy groceries for the week, or just to socialize on the streets. Consequently, beginning on Friday afternoon, the number of farmers and mill hands in town increased significantly, even more so on Saturday. Saturday therefore was an especially big day at Pelo's. The pool tables, reflecting the increased crowds, were active from opening until closing as mostly younger males competed with each other at billiards.

For venturesome youngsters, a visit to Pelo's on a Saturday was truly an adventure. Because there were no age restrictions, any boy who was willing to ignore the warnings that the pool hall was a deplorable place for a decent youngster to be, or, even worse, to defy openly his morally strict parents was free to enter either to play or watch. While growing up in the thirties and forties, most youngsters in Bladenboro did either one or the other or both.

Pelo's pool room was a noisy place on Saturdays. As the morning slipped away and the number of potential patrons increased, the talk and chatter escalated to a higher and higher level until it appeared from the outside that a raucous party was underway. Attracted by the inside noise, sidewalk passers-by often stopped to press cupped hands against the plate glass windows to determine the cause of the hoopla. Punctuating this din was the occasional crack of a cue ball striking a triangular rack that sent balls bolting helter-skelter around the felt-covered table and, if the player was skilled or lucky, into a side or corner pocket. Breaking the balls was inevitably followed by a mixed clamor of joy and cursing from the competing players, depending on whether one was hurt or helped by the balls dropping into the pockets. Then, after carefully studying the position of the balls and sighting all possible angles for the next shot by walking around the table, leaning forward for a closer look, and squinting down the cue stick to confirm the proper angle, the "shooter" deliberately and studiously chalked his cue tip for the shot. It was ritual behavior that observing youngsters quickly learned from experienced players. All the while Pelo walked around his domain, ready to collect the small fee he charged for each game. Pelo's pool room was not only a noisy place, it was also a smoky place. Nearly all the mill hands, who made up the bulk of his customers on Saturday, smoked cigarettes or chewed tobacco. With only a front door and a back door into the business, heavy smokers quickly filled the pool room with a smoky haze, particularly in the winter when closed doors prevented the circulation of air. Although the air was stifling, this did not stop several of the chain-smoking players from pausing to light up. With cigarettes dangling from their lips and smoke curling up into irritated eyes, they continued to chalk up and play the game. Not even the drafts from open doors reduced the air pollution for long. On such days, Pelo's pool room was not a healthy place to spend time. But for youngsters who used the hall to experiment with their first cigarettes, the thick smoke that floated lazily about while blending with the foul odors from the toilet in the rear symbolized not a health hazard but their entrance into manhood.

As noted, most church-going, respectable people of Bladenboro did not think highly of Pelo's pool hall because some activities that went on there were appalling to their sense of moral values. Conversations were not limited solely to the game of pool. To vent their feelings and frustrations about work in the cotton mills and the war, many players did an awful lot of loud "cussing" and swearing that could be easily heard on the outside sidewalks--language that was laced with expletives that went far beyond the "damns," the son-ov-a-bitches," and "hells" that most residents heard only occasionally in everyday conversation.

Worst of all, sex in all its forms was a favorite subject of discussion, especially among those players who boastfully claimed to be sexually active and who gloried in revealing in graphic details their alleged exploits with certain local girls who were said to be "putting out." Fascinated, envious, and sexually inexperienced listeners hung on every word, perhaps not realizing that ninety-nine percent of what they were hearing was pure fiction.

Furthermore, the presence of rowdies and the occasional fights did nothing to reduce the local anxieties about Pelo's place. Although nothing extraordinary had happened in the pool hall since the violent episode noted above, knowledgeable parents remained aware that the atmosphere there was conducive to disagreements and potential violence in which cue sticks might be used as deadly weapons. Adding to this apprehension was the character of Pelo's clientele. It consisted principally of young workers from the mill villages west of town. Unfortunately, in the late thirties and forties, among town residents mill hands from the villages had an unsavory reputation for brawling and violence. Therefore, the arrest of any inebriated young mill hand in the pool room, although infrequent, only confirmed the worst judgment of town parents about the character of the pool room and the mill people. Consequently, in the minds of many locals, even responsible parents from the villages who were fully aware of the dangers, there was always the possibility that a brawl at Pelo's might end in disaster for a loved one.

Furthermore, it was an open secret that petty gambling also occurred at Pelo's, especially on the weekends following paydays at the Bladenboro Cotton Mills. Money was openly exchanged between winners and losers, with no attempt to conceal the activity. Of course, the prevalence of known gambling did nothing but further enhance the disreputable reputation of Pelo's place among the town's respectable elements. Gambling was a good enough reason to warn their sons never to enter Pelo's for fear of moral corruption and a stained reputation. Nevertheless, although illegal, town authorities tolerated the violations, perhaps because the stakes at the tables were never very high and directly involved only a few players on the weekends.

A few of the players who gambled (usually young mill hands) remained at the game for hours playing "odd-ball," with each odd ball pocketed after the break being worth a nickel, sometimes a dime. Skilled players, who were able to run the rack, easily picked up extra dollars during the course of an afternoon, stopping only to eat hurriedly and to use the smelly toilet in the rear. The result was that the winner in these games usually occupied a table until either he tired or ran out of onlookers willing to step forward and risk their nickels and dimes by matching their skill against his. It seemed that there were always foolish challengers (usually individuals not particularly skilled at the game) eager to replace a loser only to become, in most cases, losers themselves.

Among the most skilled players who played pool at Pelo's was a young man with the surname of Bryant. At another time and place--and with opportunity--he might have become a great professional. He was certainly the best of the lot hanging out on the weekends at Pelo's. Bryant was a tall, lean fellow who could do the most remarkable things with a cue stick and billiard balls. At one time he had been injured in a hunting accident that left him badly scarred on the left side of his face. However, his vision, co-ordination, and nerves had definitely not been affected. Playing odd-ball with Bryant for money was asking to be taken to be cleaned. He took on all comers, even individuals like Allen Cox who were known locally to be highly skilled at the game. He rarely lost. Weekend after weekend, he defeated his opponents with rare skill, thereby supplementing his income by perhaps five or six dollars a week. Bryant, Cox, and a few other local "sharks" with less skill consistently picked up pocket change from the suckers who seemed anxious to lose their money.

Most of the young men growing up in Bladenboro during the forties did not "hang out" at Pelo's pool room, although it was one of the few places where one might do so. Generally, they obeyed their parents and avoided being seen there. Nevertheless, for the many youngsters who dared to risk their reputation by entering the rectangular room behind the large, plate glass windows on which was painted **Pelo's Pool Room** in large, yellow block letters, life was certainly more exciting, made more so by the fear of being discovered and reported to disapproving parents.

Clustered in the rear near the third table and the foul smelling toilet, youngsters played pool with one eye on the balls and the other on the front door, ever ready to bolt out the rear door if it became necessary to avoid detection. Faced with an angry parent, some did so. For it was not unheard of for parents, upon hearing that a disobedient son was "shooting pool," to enter Pelo's and pull the embarrassed offspring onto the sidewalk and administer a public tongue lashing. Nevertheless, in spite of its bad reputation, it is doubtful that one's moral character was forever ruined by sneaking in and playing pool at Pelo's. There were just too many other positive factors in Bladenboro that helped to offset this slight deviation from parental expectations, as evidenced by the number of young men from the town and the mill villages who turned out well. Nevertheless, one certainly learned much about life at Pelo's that could not be learned elsewhere in the town. In a strange sort of way, the stifling smoke, the clamoring voices cursing and yelling, the squeak of chalk on cue tips, the crack of balls, the infrequent fights, the awful smell from the toilet, the comradery with pool-playing friends like Sydney Edwards, J. C. Bennett, Harold Bullard, Lynwood Edwards, and Ted Shaw, the assertion of independence--all made Pelo's pool room a memorable place that contributed significantly to a young man's informal education.

Chapter 11

Putting Out the Fires: The Boro's Volunteer Fire Department

In small towns like Bladenboro, there was always the possibility of dangerous, destructive fires. Unfortunately, many of these communities had absolutely no fire protection. For example, Bladenboro did not acquire a community water and sewer system until the mid-thirties when it, like other small towns, became a beneficiary of Franklin D. Roosevelt's New Deal efforts to provide infrastructure and resulting jobs in such places. Until then in Bladenboro, only a few private citizens provided a measure of protection for themselves I recall that one of the more substantial citizens on Front Street built his own small water tower in the rear of his property that might have provided, in the event of a fire, limited water service to his and several homes of relatives who lived within its shadow. Even after the acquisition of its water system, the town failed to provide for a regular fire department with a well-trained force of paid personnel. It lacked the resources to do so. So, when fires occurred in the thirties and forties, controlling and suppressing the conflagrations was left to a volunteer group of ill-equipped citizens who did the best they could with what they had under difficult circumstances.

In constructing the town's water system, it was necessary to build a substantial water tower with tank, and the site selected for its location was a small plot behind the Women's Club House and in front of Oak Bullard's home. (For years Bullard supervised all the town's maintenance work.) As part of its fire-fighting strategy, the town attached a siren to the upper structure that was blown in an intermittent series of ear-splitting blasts in the event of a fire or other disasters in order to alert the volunteer fire fighters and the community that there existed a problem. Consequently, the central location of the tank, although not originally planned with fire-fighting in mind when selected, served the community well because the alarm, once activated, could be heard far beyond the incorporated town whose boundaries were then limited. At the sound of the siren, if during daylight hours, the volunteers hurriedly left their jobs, mostly in the local retail businesses, and assembled for action under the direction of an informally chosen leader. By the late forties, the town had acquired a beat-up, used fire truck from some source that from the looks of it, may have been a detriment rather than a help in fighting fires. It made an awful lot of noise with the roar of its engine and its siren blaring when running down Front Street while, at the same time, providing much excitement for onlookers.

The men who were members of this volunteer fire brigade provided their time and effort as a public service and, as I suspect, probably as a means of providing occasional excitement to humdrum lives. I don't recall all the names of all the men, mostly younger men of the town, who composed this group of amateur firefighters. C. A. Shaw, a managerial fixture of Bridger's Drug Store, was a member who took great pride in the town and its history. One summer day while having a soda in the drugstore the siren on the water tank went off with a series of blasts, causing C. A. to rush from the store. Shortly thereafter the ancient, red fire truck came roaring down Front Street and through the town. Hanging on for dear life were four or five men who seemed to be having the time of their lives. As it turned out, when C. A. returned he informed his customers that it was just a practice run to stir up a little excitement in the town on a lazy summer afternoon–which the exercise certainly did. For the town's siren combined with the noisy fire truck brought everyone onto the streets wondering what had happened. I recall that Roy Lennon, who worked in the Bridger Corporation Store, was also a member of this volunteer group. And Julian "Tater" Shaw, who worked for the town, was one of the most enthusiastic members of the volunteers. When the war ended in 1945, men began returning to the Bladenboro area from military service. Some of them, like Charles Herring, were residents of the town and volunteered to protect it from fires. Although infrequent, fires did occur that despite the best efforts of the volunteers, did great damage in the town. Before leaving Bladenboro for military service in 1951, there were several memorable fires, two that were unusually damaging for the town.

The first of these fires impacted indirectly on many Bladenboro students. One of the few recreational centers in Bladenboro was the high school gymnasium and the adjacent ball park. The gymnasium had been built during the thirties, part of the recovery program known as the New Deal of the Franklin D. Roosevelt administration, built as a Public Works Project (PWA) with Work Progress Administration (WPA) labor. As I remember the building, it was a soundly constructed structure, very basic building. It was nothing like the modern athletic facilities that are today located at virtually every high school. It was a totally wooden structure with pine flooring. However, although it wasn't much by modern standards, it was a building that made possible boys and girls basketball teams and physical education classes. Furthermore, there was a ramp that connected the gym to an adjacent baseball park and grandstand where both the high-school team and the Bladenboro Spinners played their baseball games and high-school football games. As described elsewhere, the ballpark grandstand was also made of wood, with changing rooms underneath. And around the park was a wooden fence that had long been weathering. Unfortunately, when not in use the grandstand was accessible to anyone, the gym less so. For boys and girls who were moving through the grades and who wanted someday to be a part of either the school's baseball, basketball, or football team, and who attended nearly every sporting event in the gym and ball park, these facilities, although not fancy, were still of great importance because of their desire to perform there as part of a school team. It was such aspirations that made the destruction of the gym and ball park such a personal disaster for many of us.

Sometime during the summer of 1943 word rapidly spread throughout the community that Bladenboro High School was on fire. Hearing the fast moving rumor, I rushed to the scene to find that it was not the high school but the gym, grandstand, and wooden fence that were ablaze. Apparently, the fire had begun in the grandstand (not a surprise because in off-seasons its underneath was always filled with scattered paper and other trash), which was smoldering when I arrived, while the gym was furiously burning. Fighting the fire were several volunteer firemen wrestling with one extended fire hose that ran behind the high school and across the Whiteville road to where a hydrant was located. With such inadequate equipment, there was no way that the gym could be saved. And while watching the volunteer firemen desperately work to save the gym, the hose suddenly lost pressure and that allowed the fire to burn even more fiercely as it blazed away on the wooden structure. (Word spread throughout the crowd of onlookers that the reason the water pressure on the hose had dropped was because a prominent citizen returning to town from Whiteville had insisted that the hose be disconnected so that his car might pass.) Of course, by the time the alleged interruption had occurred, saving a functional gym was already an impossibility. It was too far gone.

The destruction of the gym, grandstand, and ballpark fencing had long range implications. The nation was in the midst of World War II and its entire resources were being marshaled to winning that conflict–and, of course, that included the assets of our town and county. Under the circumstances of war, what had been lost could not be immediately replaced. The school's sports program (for example, football), other than intramural sports, had already been canceled. Competitive sports against other high schools were not resumed until after the war, beginning in the Fall of 1945. Then the renewal of football and baseball, although getting off to a rough start, managed reasonably well without the facilities destroyed by the fire. But basketball was different without the gym, and Bladenboro's teams, which regularly practiced on a dirt court with homemade goals and occasionally worked out in a gym in nearby Clarkton, were always disadvantaged in competing with other schools. It was years before the school authorities built a new gymnasium for the students at Bladenboro. However, for the boys and girls of my generation the fire was very hurtful.

The volunteer firemen who worked so hard to save the gym with their limited equipment did the best they could with they had at their disposal. It is unlikely that even a far better equipped, organized fire department could have saved the wooden buildings once the fire was underway. Once started, a fire in the seasoned lumber of the old gym, grandstand and fence would have been extremely difficult even for professional firemen to stop. The fire pointed to the need for better fire protection in the town. Despite their willingness to serve the community, it was obvious that an untrained group of volunteers could not provide adequate fire protection.

The other most damaging fire occurred in the in the immediate post-war forties. Prior to the fire, the Bridger block, an L-shaped two-storied edifice, extended from mid-town along Front Street beginning with the Bank of Bladenboro and running southward to the Bridger Drugstore, where it turned abruptly westward along a then unnamed street and ending with the U. S. Post Office. A substantial portion of the towns economic life occurred in this structure. For example, between the bank and the post office were a number of small businesses–the local bank, an upstairs dentist office, a furniture store with a second-floor casket showroom, a grocery store, a barbershop, a drugstore with a doctor's office, a dry cleaners, a beauty shop, the post office, and upstairs, accessed by a stairwell from Front Street, the central offices of the Bladenboro Cotton Mills, then the major enterprise in Bladen County. Consequently, the complete destruction of the Bridger block either by fire or other means would have been, at the very least, an economic disaster for the town.

From my home on NC 211 adjacent to the White Oak Original Free Will Baptist Church, I had two walking routes to Bladenboro High School. One, a short-cut that required crossing over the Seaboard Airline Railroad trestle, walking over foot-logs through Bryant Swamp, following a path along the Bridger field next to my Great Uncle Jim Hester's house to reach Back Street, and then diagonally crossing a large empty lot belonging to Henry White to Front Street near the school. The other walking route was to follow NC 211 to Front Street with all its beautiful homes and follow it south to the school. This route was much longer and I rarely walked this way unless I had plenty of time and the weather was nice. It was one of those days when I took the second route that I came across what was probably the most damaging fire experienced by the town until that time.

Apparently, the fire had begun sometime before daylight in the western end of the Bridger block. It was here that the post office, with Rob Bridger as postmaster, was located. Sandwiched between the post-office and Elizabeth Dunn's beauty shop, was one of the town's two dry-cleaning establishments. Rumors circulated that the fire had started there. Above these enterprises was located unoccupied space used principally for storage and accessible by a set of outside stairs.

These businesses within the Bridger block were separated from the rest by a firewall that turned out to be a godsend for the remaining businesses in the block. Without it all the stores and mill offices therein would have been threatened by the fire and possibly lost. Such a loss would have been catastrophic. For example, the loss of the central offices and records of the Bladenboro Cotton Mills, the largest employer in the county, would have thrown into disarray the industry that undergirded the economy of not only Bladenboro but the entire county. Nearly as damaging would have been the loss of the Bank of Bladenboro.

Upon my approaching town, it was evident that something major had happened. Smoke continued to billow upward and after crossing the Highway 211 bridge I could see the smoldering remains of the postoffice and people standing off and looking at the the burned-out site. When I arrived, the fire continued to smolder but whatever action had been taken to control the blaze was over. It is likely that the local volunteer firemen were responsible for containing the fire. If so, I didn't see them in action because I had arrived too late. Although fascinated by this scene of the results of the biggest fire in my memory, I hurried on down Front Street because I did not want to be late for school.

As one can imagine, the loss of the town's postoffice was a major loss to the town. Other than rural delivery everyone in Bladenboro had always acquired his mail either by renting a box or at general delivery. There was no home delivery available. The destruction of the facility made it necessary to locate it elsewhere. Before long, the residents began receiving their mail in an available building owned by James A. Bridger located on Front Street across from the depot of the Seaboard Railroad and adjacent to the Women's Club house. If the fire that had burned the old postoffice had originated in the adjacent dry cleaners, as some suspected, it was ironic that the restored postoffice was relocated adjacent to another dry cleaning establishment owned by James Robinson, a respected black man whose business catered to clients on Front Street. I am not certain whether Elizabeth Dunn's beauty parlor ever reopened in another part of town. If she did so, I don't recall ever seeing its location. And the dry cleaning establishment was gone. Unfortunately, the section of the Bridger block that had been destroyed by the fire was never reconstructed. As a consequence, today there remains an unattractive gap where thriving businesses once stood. However, before the end of the forties, on the west end of that street, a new dry cleaning establishment opened, owned and operated by Jodie Bennett, and a grocery store, owned and operated by J. Hinson, also opened and both continue until the present day under different ownership. The fire that destroyed the postoffice, the dry cleaners, and beauty shop demonstrated again the need for better fire protection in the town. Quite clearly, ill-equipped volunteer firemen were not up to the task of providing the level of fire protection needed.

Another fire occurred in the late forties within the town limits that had less impact on the general population but was financially hurtful to the city's major mercantile business. The Bridger Corporation store, occupied a large brick building on Front Street directly across from the Bridger Block. One of the earliest businesses in Bladenboro, its wooden structure was replaced by brick in 1908. It provided goods and services of all kinds to residents and farmers for miles around. It had a men and women's clothing department under the management of Graham Wilson, a household department where one could buy refrigerators, stoves, radios, pots and pans, and other items managed Bernard Ward, and a grocery department and a fresh meat counter managed by Dewey Guyton. In addition there were miscellaneous items that one could purchase there. For example, my father as a young man purchased an automobile tire from the store. A substantial part of the business, however, was selling and satisfying farmers' needs in the surrounding area. As I recall, most of the store's non-display inventory was kept on the second floor of the principal building or in an extended rectangular, wooden warehouse with a platform that ran parallel to but well back from the store and near Henry White's corral and livery stable. The Bridger Corporation store provided the basic needs of farming–plow lines, plows and other equipment, seeds, plants, fertilizer, and extended credit to cash poor farmers. It allowed farmers to purchase there agricultural needs "on time"–in other words, they could buy now and pay when their crops were harvested and sold in the Fall, particularly cash crops like tobacco. I recall as a teenager helping a local farmer "put in" his tobacco by working as a "hander" to a "stringer" under a barn shed and my wage of seventy-five cents for the day's work was paid in merchandise from the Bridger Corporation store, my purchase there being charged to the farmer. In those difficult times, I suspect that such arrangements were not unusual for local farmers.

Like the fire that had destroyed a section of the Bridger Block, the blaze in the warehouse of the Bridger Corporation in the mid-forties apparently began before daylight in the early morning hours. Apparently, it was well underway when discovered. Like the gymnasium fire, this was another case where volunteer firemen apparently had little chance of success in either controlling or suppressing a fire that ran wildly through seasoned lumber. Their futile efforts failed to stop the uncontrolled burning of the warehouse.

On the morning of the fire as I crossed the NC 211 bridge when approaching town while en route to school, I saw substantial smoke rising from behind the Bridger Corporation store. Altering my route, I swung around to where bystanders were milling about looking at the smoldering, burnt out remains of the warehouse and its ruined contents. There did not appear to be anything left of any value to anyone. Having satisfied my curiosity, I hurried on to school. Once again, the warehouse fire demonstrated anew the vulnerability of the community to fire. The town had received another lesson in the consequences of unpreparedness to deal with such disasters. It was soon to receive two other lessons in fires of a lesser scale that also pointed to the need for a more organized effort at fire protection.

The financial impact of its warehouse loss to the Bridger Corporatiion and its customers, especially the area farmers who relied on the store for needed supplies, was undoubtedly great but replaceable. However, for whatever reason store owners decided not to replace immediately this part of the business. Like the destruction of a portion of the Bridger Block that had left a yawning gap where the old postoffice and two other businesses had once operated, the burning of the warehouse also left a similar conspicuous, empty space that even today is a reminder of the destructive fire for those old enough to remember it.

There were two other smaller fires in the late forties that occurred within the town limits. One of them involved a small business owned and operated by Blanco Duvall. Duvall was the father of Mack Duvall, one of my schoolmate friends. Duvall was a recognized figure around Bladenboro, a man usually seen either smoking or chomping on the butt of a smelly cigar. His store where he sold fish, chickens and other items was located in the heart of Bladenboro on NC 211, directly across the highway from Azzie Hardin's barbershop, D. H. Russ's general store, and Dan Freeman's clothing store. The fire that destroyed his shop also started in the early morning hours. Like the burning of the warehouse of the Bridger Corporation, I discovered the smoldering results of the fire en route to school. Although a much smaller blaze than the other fires discussed above, the end result was the same–total destruction of the small store. The loss must have been devastating to a small-time entrepreneur who, in the past, had sold fish and vegetables on the two mill villages, and even at the time of the fire, together with his wife, had a struggling on-going business of raising and selling chickens and eggs. I do not know what role, if any, that the volunteer firemen played in the Duvall fire. Because of the total destruction, I concluded that there was nothing that they could do to save the business after the fire had been discovered.

The other fire involved a house located on NC 131, directly across from the Bladenboro High School. Because the blaze occurred so close to the school where I was a student, and, unlike the others, it occurred in the mid-daylight hours, it was the first one that I actually observed the town's volunteer firemen in action. Being so close to the school, the fire naturally attracted the attention of students who were enjoying the lunch hour outside. We watched as volunteer firemen attempted to save the small house.

A single fire hose was connected to a nearby hydrant, the same one to which a lone hose had been connected at the time of the gymnasium and ball park fire. While some volunteers placed ladders to access the roof where small wisps of smoke were beginning to appear, a couple of men laboriously tugged the hose into position and soon a stream of water was gushing against the house. Meanwhile, the work of the men on the roof, who had been busily chopping holes into the attic, unfortunately seemed to cause the fire to fiercely flourish. It soon became clear that the inside fire had progressed to the attic where flames now escaped through holes which the amateur firemen had chopped in the roof. Directing water from the hose to the roof was not immediately effective in squelching the flames. It soon became obvious that these dedicated volunteers would not be able to stop the inferno before it had done major damage to the house. Before returning to class, some students had concluded that the work of the volunteers had accelerated the fire storm inside the house. However, it was also clear that without some intervention, the house would have been entirely consumed by the flames. Emerging from school at the end of the day, we found the house smoldering, not totally destroyed but clearly unlivable because of fire, water, and smoke damage. Despite their enthusiasm in fighting the fire, the intervention by the volunteer firemen had not been able to save the house. There were undoubtedly more fires that occurred in and around Bladenboro that led to further action by the volunteer firemen. However, these are the ones that occurred during the thirties and forties.

After leaving for military service, the family reported in letters that numerous fires, probably the result of arson, occurred in unoccupied houses on the two mill villages of the Bladenboro Cotton Mills located about a half-mile to the west of town off NC 211. Like other family owned cotton mills throughout the South that were disposing of their villages because foreign competition was making textile production unprofitable, the owners of the local mills decided to rid themselves of their villages as mill owners had done elsewhere. To rid themselves of the expense of maintaining their village houses, the mill owners generously offered any worker or former worker–even outsiders such as Sidney Britt, a local farmer-businessman–a house or houses on the condition that the structures be removed off mill property. For example, my family, thinking that they could dismantle a house and use its lumber to build another elsewhere, was given a house on the Old Mill village. However, my mother made the mistake of placing a "KEEP OUT" sign on the property. The vacant house was promptly torched together with several others there.

What role, if any, the Bladenboro volunteer fire department played in fighting this outbreak of fires is not known to me. At the time (the early fifties), the villages were probably not incorporated into the town–as their former sites later were–and thus the volunteers may not have felt any responsibility for fighting fires outside the town's jurisdiction. However, the rash of fires undoubtedly added more urgency to the perception that the residents of Bladenboro needed and deserved better fire protection than it had by relying solely on amateur volunteers.

Chapter 12

Bridger's and Hutchinson's Drugstores

No one could grow up in Bladenboro without recognizing the important role that its two drugstores played in the everyday life of the town. For like the public schools and the numerous churches, the drugstores were indispensable institutions that directly affected the daily lives of nearly everyone who lived in the larger Bladenboro community. Sooner or later everyone found it necessary to enter one of these establishments that provided such vital services to residents in and around the town. Each drugstore had something about it that made it very different from the other. Nevertheless, despite the distinctive character of each, the two were remarkably similar in their impact on the community.

Owned by Dr. Dewey H. Briger, Bridger's Drugstore (usually called by its full name because of several other Bridger-owned establishments in the town) sat on the southwest corner of Front and Railroad streets. Directly across Front Street to the east was the Bridger Corporation store, and to its south directly across Railroad Street and the tracks of the Seaboard Railway was the depot. Like the Bank of Bladenboro, Ed Lewis' Furniture and Casket Store, Tom Hales's Grocery, Charley Bell's Barbershop, Elizabeth Dunn's Beauty Shop, a dry-cleaning establishment, the U.S. Post Office (until it burned sometime in the forties), and the upstairs offices of the Bladenboro Cotton Mills, Bridger's Drugstore was located in the so-called Bridger Block, a two-story brick structure that fronted both Front (east) and Railroad (south) streets.

Hutchinson's Drug Store (usually shortened to Hutchinson's), was owned by Dr. S. S. Hutchinson and was located near the intersection of NC 211 and Front Street, the town's only intersection with a stoplight. Directly across Front Street to the west was the Hutchinson Block, a two-story brick structure that housed at times a hotel, a corner cafe, W. G. Fussell's Lyric Theater, and Ally Page's Restaurant. On the north side of Hutchinson's was a filling station operated by Arthur Waterson and the small law office of Lloyd Elkins, and across Highway 211 to the north was the Bridger Motor Company of James A. Bridger. J. M. Vaught's Cash Store lay contiguous to the south.

Located on diagonal corners in the same block of Front Street, the two competing drugstores were dimensionally about the same in size and shape, and, with a few major differences, they generally stocked the same brands of over-the-counter health and other products. Each had a soda fountain with a marble top where one might refresh oneself with ice cream, soft drinks (usually Coca-Cola), and milk shakes served in glasses. And each had seating for customers who preferred to enjoy their refreshments inside. At Bridger's Drugstore, two booths nestled against the plate glass window facing the depot of the Seaboard railroad. There one could sit in comfort, watch the sidewalk traffic, chat with friends, enjoy a Coke, and view all the goings-and-comings of passenger and freight trains, which invariably triggered a lively activity around the depot and the railroad crossing on Front Street. At Hutchinson's, such pleasurable outside viewing was not possible. Its seating consisted of two small round glass-top tables with several uncomfortable wire-backed chairs that sat in a small space in front of the soda fountain toward the rear of the store. Surrounded by counters, one's view while sitting was restricted to the center-aisles, the space around the soda fountain, and the inside entrance to the medical offices of Dr. Hutchinson. Compared to that at Bridger's Drugstore, the seating at Hutchinson's was not inviting and therefore was rarely used except by Dr. Hutchinson himself. For most of the thirties and forties, however, except for the weekends when nearly everyone came to town there was not extensive use of the seating facilities in either drugstore.

Each physician owner practiced medicine and dispensed medications in offices and pharmacies located at the rear of his drugstore. To seek treatment from Dr. Bridger, a patient entered his square-shaped waiting room through either a side door off Railroad Street or an inside door from the drugstore. This room was very small and starkly furnished with two short, uncomfortable oak benches that provided limited seating. Hanging on the wall facing the entrance from Railroad Street were Dr. Bridger's framed degrees, one from Wake Forest College and the other from Jefferson Medical College. Hanging on another wall where all could see was the well-known framed picture of a very concerned physician bending over a sick, bed-ridden child in a dimly lit room. Beneath the picture was a printed letter (framed for all to see) from a patient apologizing to his doctor for the long delay in paying a bill because other financial obligations had been given priority. The message was clear: payment to one's doctor for essential services to loved ones ought to be paid first, not deferred until after all other bills had been paid.

In Dr. Bridger's waiting room, democracy prevailed. It was not segregated as was the waiting room across the tracks at the depot. For unless there was an urgent emergency, patients or accident victims, regardless of color, saw the doctor on a first-come, first-served basis. There were no appointments. If patients sat, they sat together on the oak benches.

Adjacent to the waiting room was an even smaller room that was used for initial consultation, for the patient files that Dr. Bridger maintained, and for administrative purposes such as the formal billing that was initiated after the World War II. Beginning sometime in the mid-forties, this room was occupied by Gwynn Deaver, an efficient nurse, and Raymond Gainey, a bookkeeper. Adjacent to it was an examination room. It too was starkly furnished, having the usual threatening stainless steel table with its ankle and arm clasps, a stainless steel stool, a chair, and a small stainless steel table whose top was covered with a sterilizer, rolls of tape, surgical instruments, bottles of Merthiolate, iodine, Mercurochrome, and throat swabs. The waiting room, the consultation room, and the examination room were in such close proximity that there was virtually no privacy for the patient unless the doors were closed, which was not often, especially in the hot summer months. At such times, while in the waiting room, one could easily hear the most private exchange between a patient and the doctor, or, the hurtful moans from a patient undergoing a painful procedure such as lancing a boil.

Between the examination room and the drugstore was another small room that Dr. Bridger used as his pharmacy. It was here that he stored his chemicals and medications; it was here on a small counter that he, switching to the role of pharmacist, mixed prescriptions for his patients. Large brownish, corked jars filled with foul smelling liquids, canisters filled with pills, medicine bottles of varying sizes, and small bins of corks and pill packages--all were found in this hideaway room that opened to the back counter aisle of the drugstore. (Perhaps as a favor to small boys, in the thirties Dr. Bridger paid one cent for each returned medicine bottle that had been washed sparkling clean.).

For approximately forty years in these very small quarters at the rear of Bridger's Drugstore, quarters that were not much larger than the living room of some modern homes, Dr. Bridger ran a successful medical practice. Throughout the decades of the Great Depression and World War II and continuing until ravaged by old age and bone cancer, he served well the people of Bladenboro, the nearby mill villages, and the surrounding area.

Like Dr. Bridger, Dr. Hutchinson located his medical practice at the rear of his drugstore. His rectangular-shaped waiting room was also small and starkly furnished with a long, uncomfortable oak bench that faced a window in his office. Patients entered his waiting room by either passing through the drugstore from Front Street, or by entering through a side door that faced NC 211. Once inside, they sat facing the door leading into Dr. Hutchinson's offices. Like Dr. Bridger's facilities, one room was used for office management and consultation, another for examining patients, and another for formulating medicines that he personally dispensed. In these cramped quarters, Dr. Hutchinson practiced medicine for decades, until age forced him into retirement. Older than Bridger, Hutchinson was at the peak of his medical career when the younger Bridger, just out of medical school, set up his practice in Bladenboro in the early twenties. As a result, customers at Hutchinson's in the thirties and forties were likely to see Dr. Hutchinson, his head conspicuously bald and with time on his hands from a dwindling practice, standing behind a counter or meandering around in his store, always ready to strike up a conversation with anyone who had time to talk.

The individual who managed Bridger's Drugstore was C. A. Shaw who began working there as a very young man. With the exception of a few years following Dr. Bridger's death, C. A. remained at the drugstore until his retirement. When George Edwards, a bona fide pharmacist, acquired ownership of the store, C. A. returned to work part-time until his death.

Throughout his lifetime, C. A. was a familiar fixture who was known to everyone in Bladenboro. A tall, thin, angular man who, until his later years, constantly smoked cigarettes, C. A. was a man who lived and breathed the history of his hometown. Born and reared there, he took an early interest in it and its people. Working behind the counter at the drugstore, he astutely observed the ebb and flow of town life through several decades. He became well acquainted with the mill hands, farmers, clerks, students, and local businessmen who inevitably entered the store either to purchase items or to visit the offices of the doctor in the rear. Consequently, he became an avid collector of photographs, stories, and other memorabilia that he carefully preserved for later generations. C. A. often displayed individual items (for example, a photograph of a flooded Front Street during one of many great floods Bladenboro endured prior to the WPA's ditching of Bryant Swamp in the thirties) from his collection as a means of provoking animated conversation about the town's past. Like Walter Singletary, an old gentleman who was a genealogical encyclopedia concerning the histories of families and their marital connections in southern Bladen County, C. A. was a repository of knowledge about the lives of virtually everyone living in his town. And he especially loved to talk about those people and the events that had shaped the community.

Although over the years he was assisted by various helpers, among whom were Dorothy Lennon, wife of Roy Lennon who clerked in the Bridger Corporation store across Front Street, and Eunice Guyton, whose father Emmett ran the company store of the Bladenboro Cotton Mills west of town, it was C. A. who stamped his personality on the store and made it an interesting and lively place to visit. For example, at the soda fountain, he offered two varieties of milkshakes--one with ice cream and the other with only ice--with flavors to suit a customer's taste. Of course, the first was a true milkshake and cost a dime, a nickel more than the other. The second was nothing more than flavored milk and cracked ice that he stirred with the shaker, creating the illusion that one was receiving the real McCoy. Nevertheless, youngsters without the means to order ice cream fully appreciated the equal treatment

C. A. gave to their shakes and to them. And on a hot summer day, his fountain Cokes made with syrup and served in traditional Coke glasses with a straw always seemed to taste better than the bottled ones found in the iced drink boxes of area filling stations. Sitting near the plate glass window with drink in hand watching life flow lazily by was indeed a pleasurable and memorable experience, an experience enjoyed by nearly every youngster who grew up in Bladenboro. C. A.'s chatter on subjects ranging from events in town to Jessie James, the Missouri outlaw in whom he had taken a strong interest, helped to make Bridger's Drugstore a favorite stop for young people.

Adding to that pleasure in the late thirties was a Victrola console, an old, wind-up type record player that stood in the rear of the drugstore near the inside exit into Dr. Bridger's waiting room. With it was a small collection of worn records that C. A. occasionally played. Thus in the summertime with the doors open, a passers-by might hear music emanating from the store. However, the music was not the kind that one normally heard in Bladenboro, whose residents seemed to favor that produced by Nashville's Grand Ol' Opry on Saturday night, nor the kind of black music that one might hear being played in the five-and-ten stores in Lumberton, a larger town thirteen miles to the west. In C. A.'s limited collection were such pieces as Guy Lombardo's "An Eighteenth Century Drawing Room." Because most customers had no knowledge of record players, the Victrola was something of a curiosity piece. Fascinated, some individuals stood and watched as the record spun round and round. Some of the more daring youngsters, with no objections from C. A., actually made a selection, cranked the machine, and then stood around listening to the music, one of the first steps in their cultural development.

In an era when few people living outside Bladenboro had telephones, many urgent communications were sent by Western Union. C. A. operated the teletype machine that the company had placed in the rear of Bridger's Drugstore. The arrival of a telegram usually signaled a significant event in the life of the receiver. C. A. had the responsibility of getting all incoming messages good and bad (for example, births, marriages, deaths) to the recipients. During the war, this was often an unpleasant task, especially when news arrived that a local serviceman had been wounded or killed in action in some God-forsaken place in Europe or the Pacific. He was the first to know of such terrible news.

Usually, routine messages were simply read to the recipient over the telephone, if a telephone was available. And there were precious few telephones in Bladenboro. In their absence, C. A. often requested a friend or neighbor to inform a recipient that a telegram had arrived and that he should drop by the drugstore and pick it up. Or, if the recipient had a next-door neighbor who possessed a telephone, C. A. might request the neighbor to call the recipient to the 'phone to hear the message. Or, if the telegram was really bad news, such as a death of a serviceman, C. A. saw that it was delivered immediately to the recipient.

Although there was never a heavy traffic over the teletype, Bridger's Drugstore nevertheless served as the town's communication center. The telegraph was the quickest means of communicating with friends or relatives in distant places. C. A.'s role was crucial in this process. As the on-site Western Union man, he was strategically positioned to learn much about the lives of town and area residents. Perhaps this is one reason why he became the foremost historian of the town.

Hutchinson's, however, was not without its charm. The personnel there remained as unchanging as that at Bridger's Drugstore. Miss Doshe Butler, who was second in command to the owner, was a permanent fixture during the thirties and forties. Like her counterpart C. A., she spent many years running the business for her doctor employer. For most customers, she seemed forever old. A good, gentle spinster, she was assisted at times by an adult (for example, Mrs. Dora Butler) or a teenager who was temporarily employed to assist on the busy weekends when mill-hands and farmers poured into town. It was not until after the Second World War that another permanent staff member was added. Dr. Hutchinson, an innovative businessman who owned drugstores in several other locations, employed a professional pharmacist in the late forties, a first for Bladenboro. A naval aviator during the war, the young man left town during the course of the Korean War, perhaps recalled back into active service.

In the late forties and early fifties, the Trailways Bus Company secured space in the rear of Hutchinson's to use for selling tickets. The company chose as its agent Mrs. Dora Butler whose only son Owen was a combat veteran of the Second World War, a paratrooper who was much involved in the European theater. Mrs. Dora, a willowy, frail-looking woman who constantly wore a worried and harried expression, operated the ticket counter while occasionally assisting Miss Doshe in the drugstore. Despite her apparent frailness, Mrs. Dora was an energetic, competent woman who seemed always in a hurry. In a age when several major bus companies operated nationally as the principal carriers of travelers, thus making long trips especially difficult to schedule in the absence of an "express" bus between major cities, she efficiently and quickly found the routes to the most obscure places in the maze of schedules located in the thick catalogues provided by the companies. With confidence she prepared tickets for every required transfer and explained where these would occur, leaving one with the feeling that the trip, especially if a long one, would be trouble free. Although hurried by nature, unless other customers were present she always had time to talk. An intelligent, friendly woman, she kept abreast of local and world affairs.

Hutchinson's, unlike its competitor down Front Street, was not a place often frequented by the young people of the town. There were probably several reasons for this, none of which had to do with the quality of its service or products. With its soda fountain situated near the rear, customers purchasing refreshments sat at tables surrounded by counters loaded with miscellaneous items. Or, they took their refreshments with them. Unlike the showcase window at Bridger's Drugstore that looked out on the Seaboard depot, post-office traffic, and a busy train-car crossing, a patron at Hutchinson's was unable to view anything but the inside of the store. There was no view of the busiest intersection having the town's only stoplight, not even a view of the pedestrian traffic in front. The location of the seating was not conducive to lingering over Cokes, shakes, or ice cream. It was not inviting for youngsters. Furthermore, Bridger's Drugstore was situated closer to the public schools that were located a half-mile south on Front Street. En route home in the afternoon, walking students (all students residing within two miles of the school were required to walk) reached Bridger's Drugstore first, especially highschool students with homes to the north of the schools. If they wanted refreshments and had money, they usually stopped there and lingered for awhile. Consequently, with their dismissal from school, C. A. caught the student trade before Miss Doshe had a chance to do so.

Although the service and the products sold at the two drugstore were practically the same, there was a public perception that Hutchinson's carried a greater variety of items than did its competitor down the street. This notion was particularly strong among male teenagers--some of whom rarely visited Hutchinson's--who gave a sexual interpretation to an advertisement that the store had posted on all highways entering Bladenboro. The signs were not particularly large, but for teenage males their message was pregnant with meaning. The signs read: **GET IT AT HUTCHINSON'S**, with the lettering in **It** being somewhat larger than that in the other words. Of course, to the male teenage mind the **IT** meant condoms or worse. However, the likelihood of any teenager purchasing condoms from a C. A. or a Miss Doshe was nil. They were more likely to obtain these items from the under-counter stock of a local gas station. However, because of the sign, it was a standing joke among male youngsters that **anything** from condoms to sex to horse collars could be purchased at Hutchinson's.

Because both Drs. Bridgers and Hutchinson often made house calls, in their absence patrons sometime asked C. A. and Miss Doshe to dispense needed medication that had been prescribed by their doctor. In some cases this was done. For example, over the years C. A. had come to know the aches, pains, ailments, and medications that Dr. Bridger had prescribed for his patients to treat these conditions. In the absence of the doctor, as an accommodation to a patron whom he knew and trusted as responsible, C. A. would refill a prescription of pills or tablets and report the same to the doctor. This was done infrequently and under unusual circumstances. As noted above, neither physician had a professional pharmacist until after the Second World War when one was employed at Hutchinson's for a while.

Like the barbershops, the clientele of the drugstores was different but less so. As a member of the family owning the Bladenboro Cotton Mills, Dr. Bridger, although not starting his practice until the twenties, became the physician preferred by many mill-hands, townspeople, and local farmers. There were probably several reasons for this development. An arrangement with the mill company allowed him to deduct his fees from the wages of the mill-hands, an arrangement that tended to tie patients to his practice, especially during the depression years when money was extremely scarce. A beneficial spin-off was that these patients then tended to patronize the Bridger Drugstore for their pharmaceutical needs. Some mill workers nevertheless retained Dr. Hutchinson as their physician. However, as he grew older and less and less able to respond to their calls at inconvenient hours in the night, some workers switched to the younger Bridger who was more physically able to respond. Thus the vitality of the doctors' medical practice impacted on the clientele of the respective drugstores. Furthermore, the residential section of Front Street was occupied by the large, extended Bridger family, and Back Street was occupied principally by individuals who worked in several local Bridger enterprises and who, if they went to church, attended the First Baptist Church on Front Street, which, at the time, was heavily influenced by an extended Bridger family. Such residents naturally tended to trade at Bridger's Drugstore. Even so, Hutchinson, an official in the long established but small Presbyterian Church in the center of town on Front Street, had his loyal "regulars" among the townspeople and the mill-hands who remained his patients and drugstore patrons until his death. For the hundreds of farmers and mill workers who filled the streets of Bladenboro on the weekends, a visit to one of these vital social and economic institutions was a must before departing for home. During the hard times of the Great Depression and the scarcities of the Second World War Hutchinson's and Bridger's Drugstore remained opened, surviving these upheavals under the same ownership until the death of the two doctors. For two generations, these interesting stores helped to shape the character of the town and its people.

Chapter 13

Sounds in the Night

One of the things that I most remember about Bladenboro in the late thirties and forties was the absolute stillness, the peacefulness, that early descended there with the coming of night. Away from the mills, the pervasive quietness was broken only by a barking dog or an occasional automobile. In the still of the night sounds carried a great distance and, to the careful listener, revealed much about the town's night life. As a boy I often awoke in the middle of the night and, unable to return to sleep quickly, lay near an open window quietly listening to the world outside. In the summertime with the windows open, that world was very close indeed. At the time (1938-1949), our family lived in a frame house adjacent to the original White Oak Free Will Baptist Church located on NC 211, about a half-mile east from town.

In reading the <u>Southeastern Times</u> of November 10, 1983, I came across the obituary of Frank Hester, Jr. It caused me to remember how free of noise the night was in Bladenboro. Frank was a few years older than I, but I remember him well from my early teens. He was a skilled automobile mechanic who worked in his father's garage north of town on the Dublin road. After the purchase of my first car, a second-hand, 1940 Chevrolet Coupe that was in something less than mint condition, he occasionally did repair work for me. In the mid-forties, Frank himself purchased a car with a muffler set-up that produced a distinctive sound, one that was easily identified once heard.

While owning the car, Frank and a friend dated two lovely young girls. For awhile these two couples double-dated on a regular basis. In the still of the night--and this came early in Bladenboro--their return home from dates was announced throughout the town by the alternate roar, popping and sputtering of the muffler on Frank's car. If awake, one could determine the time of arrival and departure from the young ladies' home, the movement of the car south on Front Street to the friend's residence, and the final leg back through town, across Bryant Swamp, and north on the Dublin road to Frank's home--all by the distinctive noise made by the car. The sound of the muffler punctuated the stillness of the night, telegraphing the going and coming of Frank's car to the community, that is, to the people who happened to be awake. I am confident that the four young people never dreamed that Frank's car was producing memorable sounds in the night.

Sydney Edwards, a high-school classmate and one of my best friends, joined the U. S. Army in 1948 and was shipped eventually out to California. Sometime in the fall of 1949 he returned home on leave. Prior to leaving California, he had bought an old 1939 Chevrolet, a rather large car with a trunk on the rear. Driving it day and night, he made it across the country in record time. Although ten-years old with lots of mileage, the car was obviously in good condition because he continued to drive its wheels off while on leave and eventually sold it to another good friend, Murray Santee, of Abbottsburg.

Sydney, whose friends called him Sam, had a devilish streak which found expression in various ways. During his leave he returned home in his car one night about one o'clock. It was another of those extraordinarily quiet nights when noises became exaggerated and traveled far. Leaving town, he crossed the Bryant Swamp bridge and headed west on NC 211. For some reason (probably to announce his presence), Sam had decided to test the backfiring capacity of his old '39 Chevy. For nearly a half-mile beyond the bridge to the Old Mill village cut-off to the Edwards' home-place, he repeatedly backfired the car, producing a series of explosions that surely awakened everyone living along the highway. As I recall, immediately after Sam had roared explosively past our home the night was shattered again by the wail of a siren as the town's night policeman belatedly gave chase. Such a racket at that hour was most unusual in Bladenboro! Afterwards, the pervasive silence returned, interrupted only by an occasional barking dog and the tinny-sounding din of the cotton mills in the distance.

There was only one sound that disturbed the deep silence of the night on a regular basis. Through a wooded area of towering black gum trees about one hundred and fifty yards behind our house lay the track of the Seaboard Railroad. Its rails ran for miles mostly parallel to NC 211, connecting such distant places as Charlotte and Wilmington. Passenger and mail trains ran through Bladenboro, one in mid-morning and one in late afternoon. Their stopping always attracted much attention. In between these runs and during the night, freight trains moved east and west. In the days before the development of significant motor transportation, much of the commercial items coming into town (for example, coal, mules, merchandise from mail order houses, machinery, and so on) were transported by train. This was such a normal activity during daylight hours that most people paid little attention to the hissing steam, the constantly clanging bell, the smell of burnt coal, and banging box cars that always accompanied the shifting of rolling stock off the main line onto the sidings both in town and at the Bladenboro Cotton Mills.

But if one happened to be awake in the early morning hours when an eerie silence lay across the land, the roaring rumble of a Seaboard night freight could not be ignored. As an eastbound train approached Bladenboro, the engineer signaled its coming with frequent warning blasts from his engine's steam whistle at the Butters crossing about two miles west of town. By the time the train reached the Richardson crossing, the night-piercing whistle and the oncoming rumble were beginning to shake the night. Approaching Pine Ridge and the cotton mills just west of Bladenboro where track crossings were more numerous, the engineer repeatedly blew his whistle while the rumbling of the freight reached a crescendo, shaking the earth and buildings as it sped eastward through the darkness toward Abbottsburg and Clarkton. As quickly as it had come, the powerful steam engine and its string of cars were gone with all their rumbling rapidly fading with the miles. In spite of the racket, the night run of the Seaboard freight was strangely comforting and reassuring to those who heard it. It was part of the rhythm of life that characterized Bladenboro in the thirties and forties and produced unforgettable sounds.

During the Second World War, James Shipman "courted" Stella Hester. James, who was in the Army Air Corps, was the son of Leland and Rachel Shipman and lived several houses east from us on NC 211, while Stella, the daughter of Bill Hester, a section hand (minor supervisor) in the Bladenboro Cotton Mills, lived near the company store on the Old Mill village. While on leave in 1943 or 1944, James visited Stella rather frequently in the evening, walking the relatively short distance along NC 211 from his parents' home to hers. His course took him past my home. The romance between the two young people was recognized by acquaintances as "serious," meaning that everyone expected that in time the two would marry. But for reasons known only to themselves, the romance fizzled and sputtered out. Out of the relationship, however, came a sound in the night that I shall always remember.

After one of his visits to see Stella, James was returning home around midnight. The night was still and calm and flooded with brilliant moonlight. As I lay awake in our front bedroom, the slightest sound from the outside could be heard. Somewhere up the road, probably near Grad and Lucy Kinlaw's house, James began to whistle the Air Corps song. And as he passed the H. C. Adcoxes and White Oak Free Will Baptist Church, he stopped whistling and began to sing, "Off we go into the wild, blue yonder, flying high into the sun," and so on. Rising, I watched him through the window as he walked down the moonlit highway dressed in his uniform. He continued to sing until he turned into the Shipman's yard. He was obviously a very happy young man, although under the wartime circumstances, the episode made me sad. I knew that he was leaving within a few days and that he might never return.

During World War II, the federal government imposed severe restrictions on the use of gasoline by persons fortunate enough to own cars. Of course, because the war immediately followed the Great Depression of the thirties, not many people in Bladenboro owned vehicles, for few could afford to buy them. The rationing of gasoline combined with the small number of cars in a rural setting to make most weekday evenings in Bladenboro extremely quiet. While sitting on one's front porch, as many people did in those days in the summertime, it was possible to hear conversations of neighbors some distance away as they talked the evening hours away, waiting for the house to cool down before retiring for the night. There was little to disturb the night other than the buzzing of pesky mosquitoes.

One evening while sitting on our front porch, I heard another sound which has lingered through the years. Our home was not far distant from that of the Bud Edwards family, an old unpainted structure with a large porch that was situated in the middle of the old Latt Edwards field less than a quarter-mile away. Living with the Edwards (Bud, Magaline, and Tommy) were Martha Prince and her daughter Suzie. Martha was a widow lady who had come out of nowhere to live first at the Edwards and later with Bill and Mollie Cain who with their son Curtis lived directly across NC 211 from us. Suzie was in her teens and, as I recall, was a quiet, attractive girl who had caught the attention of Ozell (Zeke) Hester, a son of my mother's Uncle Bob. For awhile, Ozell visited Suzie rather frequently, the two whiling away the evening hours on the Edwards' porch. An aspiring musician, Ozell often took along his guitar on these visits and together the two would attempt to harmonize on the popular country songs of the day.

On this particular night, one that was unusually quiet even for the times, the sound of Ozell and Suzie's picking and singing came floating crystal clear across the old Edwards' field. Again and again the words and music to "You Are My Sunshine" could be heard, broken and repeated here and there as Ozell polished his picking skills and the two perfected their harmony. The conversation on our porch lulled into silence as we sat and listened. It was a moment that somehow became permanently etched in memory, a pleasant, unforgettable moment from a simpler time forever lost. Occasionally I hear "You Are My Sunshine" and my mind races once more to that evening on the front porch listening to the voices of Ozell and Suzie coming across the old Edwards' field.

Located about three or four miles from Bladenboro was Bridger's mill pond which belonged to Dr. Dewey H. Bridger. Sometime during the thirties, Bridger had built a clubhouse in the pines up from the pond that was used by the Bridger clan for outings and parties. The pond was always stocked with bream, perch and other pan fish and provided excellent fishing. It was a lovely piece of property which Dr. Bridger made available to Boy Scout Troop 72 of which I was a member. As noted earlier, the troop was then led by Reverend Benjamin Orman, a Presbyterian minister whose church--then an old wooden structure--stood in the middle of town between the Lyric Theater and the Bank of Bladenboro. Reverend Orman began taking his scouts out to the pond in the mid-forties for camping trips. If there was inclement weather, we spent the night in the clubhouse.

Reverend Orman served two churches, one in Bladenboro and the other in Chadbourn, preaching at each twice monthly on alternate Sundays. As a result of this arrangement, not uncommon in rural areas for the times, he was frequently away. In his absence some of his scouts began camping out at Bridger's mill pond without Orman's knowledge and without the expressed permission of the doctor. The decision to "camp out" was often spontaneous among several members of Troop 72. Thereafter, we would pick up bedding and food after school and walk out to the pond and return the next morning in time to clean up before walking to school.

Bridger's mill pond provided memorable experiences. The nights there, especially the winter nights spent outdoors, were as beautiful and peaceful as I have ever known. Lying in the darkness on pine needle straw, one often looked up into a star-studded heaven through towering pines that swayed and murmured with every gentle breeze. In the chilled, clear air, the stars seemed uncommonly large--almost reachable with the slightest effort--and meteorites or "shooting stars" frequently streaked across the sky, stirring the imagination with old wives tales concerning their meaning and causing one to wonder at the glory and the majesty of it all. With a full moon also riding high in the sky, flooding the land with a soft, defused light, there was an extraordinary splendor and solitude that gripped the soul and fixed the moment permanently in memory.

It was on such a night that Robert Frink and I walked up the curving, sandy road through majestic pines toward the clubhouse where two friends, Sydney Edwards and J. C. Bennett, sat before a roaring fire in the club house awaiting our arrival. As we approached the clubhouse, Robert, who had brought along a 12-gauge shotgun, suggested that we announce our presence by firing off a blast from the gun. Our intent, of course, was to scare the daylights out of the two inside. Walking up to the window in front of which Sydney sat silhouetted against the light from the fire, Robert slipped a shell into the gun, pointed the barrel to the sky, and fired. The blast shattered the calm with an ear-splitting roar that reverberated through the stillness of the night. Across the pond lights came on in the house of Dr. Bridger's tenant; dogs awoke and began to bark throughout the area; Sydney, terribly shaken and angry, rushed from the clubhouse when he realized that he had been the victim of a prank. In retrospect, shattering the unexcelled beauty and solitude of the night seems almost a sacrilege. But very soon the spell of the night returned as quietness recaptured the countryside.

Sources

When I began writing this book my original intent was to write an institutional history of Bladenboro as a part of Bladen County, North Carolina. Its title was to be "An Anatomy of a Town." I had intended to explore and describe this small, Southern town's major institutions, for example, the origin and evolution of its town government, the two leading economic activities (textiles and agriculture), the churches and their differences in membership and doctrine, the public school system both black and white, and the class structure and the general nature of Bladenboro's society. However, as time went by work responsibilities and other projects interfered, pushing my plans for the Bladenboro book into the background. Another major difficulty was that of distance. I live a considerable distance from the town I intended to chronicle. To accomplish what I initially planned would have involved an extended stay in the Bladenboro area for research and doing so turned out to be impossible. The result was that I either had to drop the project entirely or greatly modify it.

Consequently, I decided to change the entire character of the book to one less marked by formal research and scholarship to one that would illustrate what Bladenboro was like to a youth growing up in a small Southern town during the turbulent thirties and forties by focusing on various aspects of life then. In doing so, personal memory rather than formal scholarship would be the tool to portray much about the town and its people during that era. Thus it was my decision to modify my original intent that led to this book–less scholarly than first intended, true, but nevertheless revealing about various dimensions of life among the people of Bladenboro. I am aware that relying on memory for a book of this sort can provoke controversy because others may remember its subject matter differently. That is expected because individuals experience the same event in very different ways.

What are the source of my memories? I have always considered myself fortunate to have grown up in a small rural-industrial town like Bladenboro during a time of depression and war that drew people together, despite their differences, as nothing else could. Consequently, because of these crises and because of its stable, limited population it was not difficult for one to know at some level nearly everyone–regardless of class, religion, gender, economic status, or race–living both within the town and the surrounding area in those extraordinary times. And, they also knew you, your immediate family, your relatives and their histories, good or bad. The result was a sea of shared collective knowledge about people who contributed to permanent memories among the more impressionable youths like myself who grew up there.

Also, I have always considered myself extremely fortunate to have had wonderful parents with diverse backgrounds–my mother was the daughter of a small entrepreneur in the saw-mill business, and my father was the son of a Columbus County patch farmer who, together with his brothers and sisters, was drawn into the textile industry as a child laborer. While growing up, I came to know many of the workers whom my father knew, their families, and, if not the names, the faces and knowledge of scores of other mill workers with whom I had contact. As a boy, frequent visit into the mill carrying meals to my father and, later, briefly working there on work permits as a teenager during the war, I came to know many workers and the conditions under which they labored. Those memories remain vivid.

Furthermore, both my parents were members of large, local families. My mother's people (Hesters and Edwards) were numerous in the community. The Hesters and their sizable families, most of whom worked in the local cotton mills, also compiled the majority of the working-class membership of White Oak Original Free Will Baptist Church, my parents' church during my youth. My growing up in this church remains indelibly in memory because my parents for many years were devoted members there and, whether I liked it or not, I was encouraged to attend and participate in practically all of its religious functions. Unlike my father's eight siblings and their spouses who worked in textiles, most my mother's Edwards siblings, with a few exceptions, were small farmers and they provided me with other contacts to the surrounding farming community. Consequently, while growing up I was surrounded by numerous aunts, uncles, and cousins with whom I had frequent contact and who provided constant impressions of different dimensions of life in the 'Boro, especially its work life.

Another important source of my memories was the Bladenboro Public Schools. I was again fortunate to have attended school during extraordinary times when the teachers in the elementary grades were hard-core professionals who tolerated no nonsense but focused on teaching and learning. Their jobs depended on their competency. What made the school years so important from the standpoint of memory was that my entering classmates and I remained together from 1935 until 1947, that is, during our entire public school career, moving up together grade by grade with the passing years until graduation. Friendships born in those early years remained firm for a lifetime, further solidified by periodic visits and class reunions over the years in which our student experiences in athletics, in classroom academics, in personal and teacher relationships during the school years were rehashed over and over. Even when discounting the embellishments that inevitably occurred in the retelling of school-day events, the retelling nevertheless served to further etch into memory the core of small-town life and its people mirrored in our lives at school.

While growing up, an important source of memories about life in Bladenboro originated in my work experiences. Like most youngsters of my generation, an introduction to work occurred very early in life. For example, on the local farms children were early put to work doing simple tasks and absorbed into the family workforce. And because of the "hard times," non-farm children also sought out any doable tasks during the summer months that would provide spending money for clothes, a movie, dates or whatever. For example, in my case "working" in tobacco–usually around the barn doing tasks like "handing" to "stingers," "unloading" trays of tobacco or "cropping" tobacco–was a late summer job for me. Occasionally, there were other farm jobs, such as "pulling" peanuts and "picking" cotton. Other jobs included digging worms in Bryant Swamp for fish bait to sell to avid fishermen, hoeing out a neighbor's garden, selling both parched and boiled peanuts on the crowded Saturday streets of Bladenboro, setting up pins in a bowling alley, selling the Grit newspaper, working as a clerk in a kiosk outside the Wilmington shipyard, several wartime stints of working in the New Mill's winding room and packing room, clerking briefly in Collins' Department Store, and delivering the Charlotte Observer for a short while on the mill villages–and, of course, maintaining our own sizable and essential garden while my father worked in the Wilmington shipyards during the war. In addition to the dab of income these jobs provided and the development of my personal work ethic, they also kept me further involved in many aspects of community life.

The job that was most enlightening and memory generating was my work in the grocery store of Bill and Charles Hussey that began on weekends during the war years, continued on weekends during my high-school years, and ended with my working full time in the summers until I left home for college. Bill, the founder of the store, was a former Swift Company salesman who had married into the dominant Bridger family of Bladenboro. He was a gregarious and highly competitive man who did not hesitate to open his store during a period of product scarcity and wartime rationing and against his major competitors, the Bridger Corporation Store and the company store of the Bladenboro Cotton Mills. He was a master salesman, selling anything he could acquire both locally and from major wholesalers such as the Thomas Howard Company out of Charlotte. As part of his grocery, his adjacent warehouse at times was filled with lespedeza hay, live chickens, hog and chicken feed, tobacco seeds, stands of lard, a barrel of molasses that he sold by pint, quart, or gallon, and, at one time, even a bushel hickory of nuts he had acquired in order to retain a customer in exchange for merchandise from his grocery. (He sold the hickory nuts at a profit to a lady customer whom he awed with a tale about how tasty and wonderful his mama's hickory nut pie used to be.) Located in Oz Hester's old bicycle shop at the town's only stoplight intersection across from the Bridger Motor Company, the Husseys' store was flooded on Fridays and Saturdays with farmers, mill workers, and blacks. Working in such an environment, I grew to know a flood of people, black and white, who came into the store–in a few cases knowing even their preference in the snuffs and chewing tobaccos that some resorted to because of the wartime scarcity of cigarettes. Talking to a customer while slicing off a piece of fatback or a slice of cheese from a wheel, or, jotting down the price of each item from a pound of beans to a can of tomatoes and adding up the total bill while the customer stood looking on and checking one's arithmetic helped me to know my patrons very well. Certainly those experiences with people while working in the Husseys' grocery are deeply etched in my memory bank.

Another source of memory was the complete freedom from fear that characterized my youthful years in Bladenboro. Unlike today when parents are constantly worried about the safety of their children from gun "nuts" who engage in mass murders, or, the prevalence of addictive drugs, or, violent racial conflict, or, the pervasive "moral decay" of today's society, my parents–and I think other parents–were not preoccupied with such persistent fear of threats to the welfare and safety of their children. In my case, the absence of such fears meant that the southern half of Bladen County, especially the area around Bladenboro, was my playground. I had no fear of selling bundled reed yard brooms and house brooms of straw door-to-door in the black community. Nor did I have any physical fear, except for dogs, when delivering the Charlotte Observer in the morning darkness in the two mill villages. And I didn't have any fearful concerns when friends and I rode our bikes out to June Singletary's millpond and the Big Swamp for swimming or fishing, or, when sleeping out at Bridger's millpond on unsupervised Scout outings. Such a healthy, wholesome atmosphere contributed to my knowing the people around me and their knowing me. The result was that wherever I was in the community–good parts or bad parts–I was confident that all would be well. That confidence helped to fixate my memories of the community for a lifetime.

In conclusion, I must pay a special tribute to my father who was alive when I was writing Chapter 1 concerning the class structure in and around Bladenboro. He had an amazing recall ability, being able to remember names, events, and marital and blood relationships and link them in a rational pattern. He was a genealogical marvel. Even in very old age when his contemporaries were deceased and he had no one with whom to share their common life experiences, his ability to relate his knowledge of the past continued to surprise me. He seemed either to know or know about everyone in the Bladenboro community, and they seemed to know him. In my infrequent returns there, I would often ask about people included in the chapter. More often than not, our memories confirmed each other. So, in Chapter 1 I owe a collaborative debt of gratitude to my deceased father while, at the same time, assuming responsibility for any faulty memory that has occurred.

Made in United States
North Haven, CT
05 July 2023

38569813R00093